HISTORY OF CHRISTIANITY

IN

INDIA;

WITH ITS PROSPECTS

HISTORY OF CHRISTIANITY

IN

INDIA;

WITH ITS PROSPECTS.

A SKETCH.

COMPILED FROM SHERRING, SMITH, BADLEY, AND REPORTS

GYAN

Published by

Gyan Publishing House
5, Ansari Road
Daryaganj, New Delhi-110002
Phone: 011-47034999, 9811692060
E-mail: books@gyanbooks.com

Distribution Network
gyanbooks.com
India, USA, Canada, UK, Australia

ISBN: 978-93-6433-322-1 (HB)
First Published, 1895

2nd Impression 2024

Printed at: Gyan Press, Delhi.

HISTORY OF CHRISTIANITY IN INDIA; WITH ITS PROSPECTS
Author: SHERRING, SMITH, BADLEY, AND REPORTS

HISTORY OF CHRISTIANITY

IN

INDIA;

WITH ITS PROSPECTS.

A SKETCH.

COMPILED FROM SHERRING, SMITH, BADLEY, AND REPORTS.

Madras:
THE CHRISTIAN LITERATURE SOCIETY.
S. P. C. K. PRESS, VEPERY.

1895.

CONTENTS.

Page.

INTRODUCTION 1

The First Christian Missionary to India... 2

The Syrian Christians in India 3

Roman Catholic Missions in India 8

PROTESTANT MISSIONS 11

First Protestant Missionaries to India 11

C. F. Schwartz 15

PROTESTANT MISSIONS ACCORDING TO NATIONALITIES 21

Bengalis 21

Early Missions, 24; English Chaplains and Bishops, 29; Missions now at work, 31; Female Education, 36; The Bramho Samaj, 37.

Assamese... 40

Nagas 41

Mikirs 43

Khasis 43

Garos 44

Lepchas 45

Oriyas... 46

Santals 48

Tribes of Chota Nagpore 51

Hindustanis 54

Rajputs 63

Panjabis 64

Tibetans 69

Kashmiris 71

Afghans or Pathans 73

Sindis 75

Gujaratis 76

Mahrattas 78

Bhils 84

Page

Gonds 8
Kois 8
Telugus 8
Tamils... 9
Canarese 10
Nilgiri Tribes 11
Tulus 11
Malayalis 11
Zenana Missions 11
Bible Translations 11
Bible Societies 12
The Religious Tract Society 121
The Christian Literature Society 12
The Salvation Army 12
Summary view of the Progress of Christianity in India ... 12
Changes effected by a Christian Government 12
Social and Moral Reforms have been promoted ... 12
Hindu Religious Ideas are being Christianised 12
The Prospects of Christianity in India 12
The Parallel between Ancient Europe and Modern India ... 1
The Change which took place in Ancient Europe ... 1
The Change which will take place in India 1
How India would be benefited by the adoption of Christianity 1
The Political Advantages 1
Material and Social Advantages 1
Moral and Religious Advantages ... ...
Index ... ...
List of Publications for Indian Readers ... ...

CHRISTIANITY IN INDIA.

INTRODUCTION.

THE history of the world divides itself into two great portions: the first, BEFORE THE COMING OF JESUS CHRIST; the second, AFTER HIS ASCENSION.

God created man holy and happy; but he soon fell from his original state, and brought ruin upon himself. Still, a gracious promise was given. Milton thus describes both:

> "Of man's first disobedience, and the fruit
> Of that forbidden tree, whose mortal taste
> Brought death into the world, and all our woe,
> With loss of Eden, till one greater Man
> Restore us, and regain the blessful seat."

Before Adam and Eve were sent out of Paradise, the promise was given that "the seed of the woman should bruise the head of the serpent," or that One, descended from Eve, would overcome Satan. Through Him we may obtain entrance to an abode far happier than the garden of Eden, with all its delights.

In many parts of the world, there are traditions of a golden age. Besides this, Hindus also expect that at the close of the Kali Yug, Vishnu will come as the Kalki *avatara* on a white horse to destroy the wicked, and restore the earth to its original purity. There are glimpses of great truths in such conceptions; but in Christianity we find their true fulfilment.

The promise of a Deliverer given in Paradise was repeated in various ways during the next 4,000 years. Abraham was told that in one of his descendants all nations of the earth would be blessed. Moses told the Israelites that God would raise up a prophet among them, like himself, to whom they were to listen.

During the next thousand years, different prophets foretold many events connected with the promised Saviour. The time was mentioned: He was to belong to the tribe of Judah and the family of David; the place was named Bethlehem; He was to be born of a virgin; He was to have a forerunner; He was to perform wonderful works, yet He was to be despised, rejected and put to death; His hands and feet were to be pierced; lots were to be cast for His garments; He was to be buried in a rich man's grave; but He was to rise from the dead, and establish a kingdom which would have no end.

The Lord Jesus Christ was born in Palestine nearly 19 centuries ago. He was crucified under Pontius Pilate, the Roman

Governor; but on the third day He rose from the dead. Before ascending to heaven He gave this command to His followers: "Go and teach all nations, and lo! I am with you alway, even unto the end of the world."

For some time the disciples of Christ zealously obeyed His parting command, and the great Roman Empire, formerly idolatrous, became in three centuries nominally Christian.

The Christian Church lost its original purity, and adopted several superstitious practices from the heathen nations around. It then ceased, to a large extent, to be aggressive; although there were always a few good men who sought to make known the Gospel.

In the following pages a short account is given of the progress of Christianity in India. To describe it fully would require several large volumes. Only a few leading points can be mentioned. For fuller details, the reader is referred to the works noted below,* which have been used more or less in this compilation.

The First Christian Missionary to India.

There is a tradition that the Apostle Thomas first brought the Gospel to India. In ancient times, India had a very wide meaning, extending from the East Coast of Africa to the islands of Japan. It was divided into Middle, Greater, and Lesser India. Possibly the Apostle Thomas may have laboured in Middle India. The Missionary Thomas, who is said to have suffered martyrdom at St. Thomé, a suburb of Madras, lived several centuries after the Apostle. From a very early period, the spices, gold and gems of India were taken to Europe. In those days the mariner's compass was unknown, and there were no accurate maps. Goods were therefore taken by a tedious land journey, merchants travelling in large numbers, called caravans, for protection against robbers. About the year 50 A.D., the pilot Hippalus discovered that the winds of the Indian Ocean, called monsoons, blow about half the year from the south-west, and the other half from the north-east. If therefore ships sailed to India by the one monsoon, they could return by the other. This led to a sea-borne trade between Egypt and India. The fleets sailing from one of the ports on the Red Sea and passing through the Strait of Babelmandeb, crossed the Arabian Sea to the South-West Coast of India, famed for its spices.

At that time, about 70 A. D., South India was divided into several independent native states; such as Pandya and Kerala in the west, Chola and Chera in the east. Their rulers wisely encouraged settlers, who enriched them by trade. They were not only protected, but had some special privileges.

---

* Sherring's *History of Protestant Mission in India*. 8vo. 478 pp. The Religious Tract Society. 6s.

Smith's *Conversion of India*. 8vo. 278 pp. Murray. 9s.

Alexandria, founded by Alexander the Great, near one of the mouths of the Nile, was the chief seat of Egyptian trade, and in population was inferior only to Rome. Under the kings of Egypt, called Ptolemies, Alexandria was famed for its learning, and had a celebrated library. Christianity was brought to it at an early period. The evangelist Mark, the companion of Paul the first missionary to Europe, and the writer of one of the Gospels, settled in Alexandria, and opened there a school for catechists. It became afterwards a training school for missionaries who went to all the countries around.

Some Indian merchants, probably Jews, who went to Alexandria to sell their spices and gems, found there something more valuable—the "pearl of great price." They became acquainted with the way of salvation through the Lord Jesus Christ. A petition was addressed to the Bishop of Alexandria for a Christian teacher to be sent to India. At that time, Pantænus was at the head of the Catechist School. Born, it is believed, at Athens, he was well acquainted with Greek philosophy, but he embraced Christianity. He was not only very learned, but a great teacher, able to acquire a powerful influence over his students, and distinguished as an expositor of the Scriptures. Under him the school attained a high reputation, and became a nursery of the Church.

The appeal to the Bishop of Alexandria to send a missionary to India reached him about 180 A.D. He wisely selected Pantænus for such an important field. Clement, an able disciple, could take his place during his absence, which made him less unwilling to leave his work at Alexandria. He would sail up the Nile for some days, then travel across the country to the port of Berenice on the Red Sea, from which the Egyptian fleets departed on their eastward voyage. The coast of Malabar would be reached in about 40 days.

How long Pantænus was in India, how far inland he travelled, and when he returned to Egypt, is not known. He found among the Indian Christians the Hebrew Gospel of St. Matthew which formed the basis of the present Greek Gospel. Pantænus returned to Alexandria, and continued to preside over the school till about 211 A.D., where he is said to have suffered martyrdom.

About a century later, a missionary, Theophilus, surnamed Indicus, visited India, where he found in some parts Christianity already planted.

The Syrian Christians in India.

Syrian Christians, on the South-West Coast of India, are so called, because their liturgy or church service, is in Syriac. This shows that Christianity came to them originally from Syria. The precise period when it was first brought to India is uncertain. The

Syrian Christians claim to have received it at a much earlier date than is admitted by European historians.* It is probably of Nestorian origin.

Nestorius, a native of Northern Syria, became so eminent that in 428 A. D., he was appointed by the Emperor Patriarch of Constantinople. Having adopted some views about the person of Christ which were condemned by the bishops of Rome and Alexandria, Nestorius was deposed and banished. But the Christian sect which followed his opinions, though shut out of Europe and Africa, flourished in Asia and sent missionaries to Persia, India, and China. In 552 A. D., Nestorian missionaries, who had gone to China, first brought the eggs of the silkworm to Europe. In 547 A. D., Cosmas, a merchant of Alexandria, who had often sailed to the East, thus bears witness to the spread of Christianity:—

"Even in the Island of Taprobane (Ceylon), in Farther India, where the Indian Sea is, there is a Church of Christians, with clergy and a congregation of believers, though I know not if there be any Christians farther on in that direction; and such is also the case in the land called Malè, where the pepper grows. And in the place called Kalliana there is a bishop appointed from Persia."†

The Indian princes of the South West Coast of India granted extensive privileges to the early Christian colonists, recorded on copper-plates still in possession of the Syrians. Their chiefs were authorised to use certain ornaments and musical instruments and emblems of authority, to collect particular taxes allotted to them, and to exercise jurisdiction over their own people. Christians were placed on an equality with the Nairs; they were the first to learn the use of gunpowder and fire-arms. They were usually placed in the van, or around the person of the prince. After a time, the ruling power passed into the hands of the Hindu Rajas.

The late Rev. S. Mateer, who resided for many years in the part of India where the Syrian Christians are found, gives the following sketch of their history in modern times:

"After the arrival of the Portuguese on the Western Coast of India early in the 16th century, the Romish priests soon discovered these people, and determined to effect their subjection to the papal authority. At first, measures of conciliation were pursued. In 1545 Franciscan friars were sent by the Archbishop of Goa to open a seminary for Syrian youths who were afterwards to be ordained as priests; but the Syrians refused to admit these to their churches.

"Resolved to effect their purpose, stronger measures are now

* See correspondence in the *Madras Christian College Magazine*. Vol. X., between a Syrian Christian and the Rev. Dr. G. M. Rae, Author of *The Syrian Church in India*.

† Quoted in Dr. Smith's *Conversion of India*, p. 29.

resorted to. Plots were laid to seize Mar Joseph, the Syrian Metran, or bishop, whose influence against Rome was very great. He was made prisoner and sent to Portugal in 1558. Another Metran, Mar Simeon, who had been sent to India by the Patriarch of Mosul, was decoyed to Cochin, sent to Rome, and tried as a heretic by the Inquisition. There is every reason to believe that he ended his days in the dungeons of the Inquisition in Portugal.

"In 1595, Alexis de Menezes, who was about to proceed to Goa as Archbishop, was directed by Pope Clement VIII., to make strict inquiry into the faith and obedience of the Syrian Bishop and his flock, and to prevent any bishops or priests from Syria reaching Malabar. Early in 1599, Menezes, attended by the Portuguese troops, reached Cochin, and summoned the Syrian Archdeacon George (the late Metran being now dead) to appear before him. The Archdeacon at first boldly refused allegiance to the authority of the Church of Rome; but was at last tired out by the perseverance and zeal of Menezes and the threats of the Portuguese power, and induced to sign an acknowledgment of the Pope's supremacy. Menezes visited in person many of the Syrian churches, but they refused to submit to his authority; with the exception of a few whom he won over by denunciations, bribery, and fraud.

"The assembling of a Council or Synod was now resolved on, that there might be an appearance of legality in the tyrannical and cruel proceedings of Menezes. This Synod met at Udiamperur, or Diamper, near Cochin, on 20th June, 1599. It was attended by the Romish Archbishop, the Syrian Archdeacon, and 153 Syrian priests, many Romish priests, and some chief persons among the Portuguese. Here the Archbishop gained his own way. By most unrighteous means decrees were passed confirming the doctrines of Rome, and repudiating those which had hitherto been held and proclaimed by the Syrian Church. But it was found necessary to consent to the continued use of the Syriac language in public worship.

"This state of things continued for about 50 years, till the iron yoke of oppression ultimately became insufferable to those who still adhered to the early faith. In 1653 many of the Syrians revolted from the Romish power, excluded the Romish priests from their churches, and appointed their Archdeacon as Metran, until they could obtain a Bishop from their patriarch. When the expected bishop, Mar Attala, at last managed to reach the shores of India, he was ensnared and sent to Goa, where he was consigned to a dungeon in the Inquisition and at last cruelly burnt as a heretic A.D. 1654."

The Portuguese had raised Cranganore to an Archbishopric. It was taken by the Dutch in 1661; thenceforward the Portuguese power declined, and the Syrians enjoyed freedom from external violence. Still, many continued to adhere to the Church of Rome, while others remained under their own bishops, connected with the patriarchate of Antioch.

The late Dr. Burnell, of the Madras Civil Service, wrote an account of three crosses in South India, with old Syriac inscriptions. The one of which a picture is given was built into the wall behind the altar in a church at the Great Mount, Madras, and discovered

OLD CROSS AT THE MOUNT, MADRAS.

during some excavations about 1547. A bird, like a dove with expanded wings, is over the cross, intended as a symbol of the Holy Ghost descending on the Lord Jesus Christ. Two other inscriptions are in the old Church at Kottayam. They have thus been translated: "Let me not glory except in the cross of our Lord Jesus Christ, Who is the true Messiah, and God alone, and Holy Ghost." The inscriptions are considered to belong to the 7th and 8th centuries. They are the oldest Christian inscriptions in India yet known.

The Syrian Churches, seen dotted along the South-West Coast of India, have sloping roofs, small pointed arched windows, and buttresses supporting the walls. Most of them are built of polished stone. Some of the bells are of large dimensions. In front of the Church stands a pedestal, on which a handsome stone cross is elevated; the whole being sometimes as much as 20 feet high. The ordinary dress of the priesthood is a long white coat of cotton cloth, tied or buttoned in front, and loose white trousers. The hair on the top of the head is shaved, but the beard is usually worn long.

The Syrian Christians were first brought prominently before English Christians by Dr. Claudius Buchanan, who visited their country in 1806. He showed the priests for the first time a printed copy of the Syriac New Testament. One of the Syrian Bishops presented Dr. Buchanan with a very ancient manuscript of the Syrian Bible, which was afterwards printed, chiefly for the use of Syrian Christians.

SYRIAC. (*Travancore, Syria, &c.*)

ܗܟܢܐ ܓܝܪ ܐܚܒ ܐܠܗܐ ܠܥܠܡܐ. ܐܝܟܢܐ
ܕܠܒܪܗ ܝܚܝܕܝܐ ܢܬܠ. ܕܟܠ ܡܢ ܕܡܗܝܡܢ
ܒܗ ܠܐ ܢܐܒܕ. ܐܠܐ ܢܗܘܘܢ ܠܗ ܚܝܐ
ܕܠܥܠܡ.

A few years later, Colonel Munro, the Resident at Travancore, applied to England for clergymen to be sent out to India, with the object of imparting instruction to the Christians of the Syrian faith. Three missionaries, the Rev. Messrs. Bailey, Baker, and Fenn, were sent out by the Church Missionary Society in 1816. The object at first was to induce the Syrian Church to reform itself from the superstitions and corruptions which had grown up in it in past ages. In this, for several years, the missionaries were supported by the Metran Dionysius. His successor was of a different disposition, and in 1838, the Church Missionaries commenced a new and independent mission, which will afterwards be described.

The Syrian Church has suffered from internal dissensions—at times rival bishops contending for supremacy. Still, on the whole, there has been progress. Many abuses which shocked the early missionaries have been removed. The priests are better educated, and do more for the instruction of their flocks.

At the census of 1891 the Syrian Christians were returned as follows:—

Travancore	176,574
Cochin	21,784
	198,358

Roman Catholic Christians in Travancore and Cochin are divided into Churches of the Syrian Rite and the Latin Rite. The former use Syriac in church services, the latter, Latin. The census of 1891 gives the total of both as follows :

Travancore	279,197
Cochin	150,229
	429,426

Roman Catholic Missions in India.

The chief object of the following compilation is to describe *Protestant* Missions in India, but a chapter will be devoted to a brief account of the early Roman Catholic Missions in that country.

The differences between Roman Catholic and Protestant Christians may be first noticed. In all religions, if men exercise their judgments, there will be diversities of opinion. There are far wider differences among Hindus, although all acknowledge the Vedas, than among Christians.

Roman Catholics and Protestants, as a rule, both accept the brief statement of Christian truth, usually called the Apostles' Creed. With regard to *most* of the essential doctrines all Christians are agreed. One great difference between Roman Catholics and Protestants is that the former acknowledge the Pope of Rome as the head of the Church, while the latter deny it. Protestants are so called because they *protested*, or made a declaration against, certain doctrines of the Church of Rome. Both Roman Catholics and Protestants receive the Bible as the Word of God, but the former assert that the Church must be the interpreter of its meaning. The Pope was also lately declared to be infallible in matters of doctrine.

The principle of religious liberty is generally held by Protestants ; they consider that force should not be employed in religion. Some Roman Catholics hold the same views, but until recently in many Roman Catholic countries no other religion than Popery was tolerated. It was considered right to imprison or put to death persons who were considered to hold erroneous doctrines. This is a remnant of heathenism. King Nebuchadnezzar threatened to throw into a fiery furnace all who would not worship the golden idol he had set up ; Jains in South India were impaled by Hindus.

One of the earliest Roman Catholic Missionaries to India seems to have been Jordanus, who was twice in India. He was sent out the second time in 1430 as Bishop of Columbum, or Quilon, on the South-West Coast. In 1498 Vasco da Gama landed at Calicut. Within the next half century the Portuguese had planted trading forts along the coasts of Western India. With them came Roman Catholic priests, some of whom laboured among the Hindus. One, named Michael Vaz, met with considerable success among the fishermen. But it was Francis Xavier who gave the great impulse to Roman Catholic Missions in India.

Xavier, of noble descent, was a Spaniard, born in 1506. He went to the University of Paris and took his M.A. degree at twenty, soon after which he was appointed to teach philosophy. There he made the acquaintance of Ignatius Loyola, formerly a soldier, but now a student. Xavier was fond of pleasure, but Loyola led him to higher things by pressing the solemn question, "What is a man profited if he shall gain the whole world, and lose his own soul?"

In 1534, Loyola, Xavier, and five others, at midnight in a chapel underground, dedicated themselves by solemn vows to God's service. A few years later Loyola, with the sanction of the Pope, established the "Company of Jesus;" the members of which are called Jesuits. The motto is, "To the greater glory of God."

Xavier wished to go as a missionary to Palestine, but he was led to India. John III., King of Portugal, was zealous for the spread of Christianity in his Eastern possessions. He applied to the Pope to send out some Jesuit missionaries to India. Two were appointed, but both falling ill, Xavier took their place. In 1541, he sailed from Lisbon in company with the new viceroy.

When Xavier arrived at Goa, he was deeply grieved by the ungodly conduct of the Portuguese settlers. How could the Hindus be evangelised while nominal Christians were such a disgrace to the name they bore? For 5 months, he devoted himself to the work of reformation. His days were spent in preaching, in catechizing the young, in visiting the hospitals. His zeal and piety won admiration, and a manifest improvement took place in the morals and conduct of the community.

But Xavier's heart yearning for work of a more directly missionary character, he went to the South. He began by getting the Creed, the Lord's Prayer, and the Ten Commandments translated into the vernacular. After committing them to memory, with bell in hand, he went through the villages, and summoned large congregations, attracting children especially by his kind words and gentle looks. To these he recited the translations, and after each article of the Creed, he asked them whether they believed. On their assent, he gave a short exhortation, and then baptized them. He wrote: "It often happens to me that my hands fail through the fatigue of baptizing, for I have baptized a whole village in a single day; and often by repeating so frequently the Creed and other things, my voice and strength have failed me."

For three years, beginning with May, 1542, Xavier toiled as a missionary in South India. He then went to the Spice Islands of the Indian Archipelago for 2½ years. On his return he spent 15 months in India, directing the labours of a number of Jesuit missionaries who had been sent out. To reform European society he sought to place good preachers in the principal towns. His next object was the conversion of the Japanese empire. After labouring there with considerable success, he returned to Goa to organise a mission to China. He met with much opposition from his own countryman, and he died in 1852 on the sandy shore of the small island of Sancian. His last words were: "O Lord, in Thee have I trusted; I shall never be confounded." His body was afterwards taken to Goa, where it is now preserved.

The best known Jesuit labourers in South India after Xavier are Robert de Nobili, John de Britto, and Father Beschi. The first commenced a mission at Madura in 1606, when it was the splendid capital of Terumala Nayak. Xavier had laboured among the poor; Robert de Nobili sought to gain over the higher castes. To succeed in this, he pretended to be a Brahman priest from Rome and a Saniyasi of the strictest profession, and assumed the name of *Tattuva Potaka Swami*. Xavier never mastered the vernacular; but de Nobili was a distinguished Sanskrit and Tamil scholar. He wrote a number of books, some of which still in use. De Nobili, after gaining a number of converts, died in a mud hut near the Church of St. Thomas, not far from Madras, attended by a few Brahmans.

John de Britto was a Portuguese nobleman who was led by the example of Xavier to become a missionary. The Brahmans, jealous at the success of Christianity, stirred up a persecution, and de Britto suffered martyrdom.

In 1714 the Madura Mission revived under Father Beschi. He conformed in his dress, food, &c., to the customs of the people, and assumed the pomp of a Hindu guru. He travelled on a white horse or in a stately palanquin; a man held a purple silk umbrella over him, another fanned him with peacock feathers. He was known as *Viramamuni*, the 'Heroic Devotee.' He was the best Tamil scholar of his age, and wrote a celebrated poem, called *Tembavani*.

Akbar, the Mogul Emperor, ascended the throne in 1556. One of his wives is said to have been a Christian, and he ordered his son Prince Murad, when a child, to take lessons in Christianity. Portuguese priests were invited from Goa, and Akbar took an interest in the discussions between them and the Muhammadans. Latterly he attempted to establish a religion of his own.

Jesuit Missionaries went as far as Nepal, which they entered in 1661. In Rome there are several translations from the Nepali.

There are now Roman Catholic Missions scattered all over India. Calcutta and Bombay have Jesuit Colleges, with a large number of professors. In South India the principal college is at Trichinopoly.

The *Madras Catholic Directory* for 1894 gives the number of European Missionaries as 619; Native priests 668; of Roman

Catholics as 1,130,489. Besides these there are the Roman Catholics in Goa, Damaun, Cochin, and Meliapur, estimated at 479,630. Including 249,437 Roman Catholics in Ceylon, the entire number is about 1,859,556.

PROTESTANT MISSIONS.

Some of the points of difference between Protestant and Roman Catholic Christians have been already mentioned. It may be added here that the northern nations of Europe are chiefly Protestants; and the southern nations, Roman Catholics. The great majority of the people of the United States are Protestants; while southward in America they are Roman Catholics.

There is also the Greek Church to which Greeks and Russians belong. It differs from the Roman Catholic Church in denying the supremacy of the Pope, in requiring priests to marry, in allowing the Scriptures to be read, and in using pictures of the saints instead of images.

First Protestant Missionaries to India.

The success of the Portuguese, led some other European nations to establish Companies to trade with India, and to seek for settlements in that country. Among them were the Danes, belonging to Denmark, a small kingdom in the north of Europe. In the year 1621, about the same time as the English formed a settlement at Masulipatam, the Danes obtained from the Raja of Tanjore the town and small surrounding territory of Tranquebar on the eastern coast of South India. To this was added Serampore in Bengal. More than 80 years elapsed before the Danes took any steps to make known the Gospel in India. Frederic IV., King of Denmark, had been educated by the Rev. Dr. Lutkens, a man of earnest piety, who had taught him to use his high position as a means of doing good. Urged by Dr. Lutkens the king wished to send missionaries to Tranquebar. Dr. Lutkens, though aged, wished to go himself, but the king said that only younger men could stand the climate. To the great grief of the king no missionaries could be found in Denmark; so they were sought from Germany where there were some earnest pious men.

Two young Germans, who had been students of the University of Halle, Bartholomew Ziegenbalg and Henry Plutschau, offered themselves, and sailed for India in November, 1705. They landed in India on the 19th July, 1706, the voyage having lasted nearly 8 months.

Europeans generally are thought to be Christians; but many are so only in name. To such Jesus Christ will say at the last day,

"I never knew you, depart from me, ye workers of iniquity." Christianity strongly condemns sin of every kind; wicked men therefore hate it and its teachers. Many of the Danes at Tranquebar in those days were leading immoral lives, and did not wish missionaries to come to the country. As soon as Ziegenbalg and Plutschau had explained their object, they were advised to make all haste home again. They showed their Commission, signed with the royal seal, but without avail. For a time they had to stand in the open street without a lodging, till some one having pity on them gave them a small house.

The two young men, strangers and friendless, mingled many tears with the prayers in which they besought God to aid them in their work. To acquire a knowledge of Tamil, they agreed with an old schoolmaster that he should teach his pupils in their house and teach them also, they taking their places in the classes with the children. Afterwards they met with a well educated Tamil, acquainted with several European languages, who became their teacher, and under whom they made rapid progress. Ziegenbalg preached his first Tamil sermon in less than a year after he landed.

At that time there were many slaves in India, some of whom were owned by Danes at Tranquebar. Ziegenbalg asked the governor that some time should be allotted every day for their religious instruction. The governor was not friendly to missionary work, but as he had lately received a latter stating that the King of Denmark was much interested in it, he granted Ziegenbalg's request. Five of these slaves were baptised in May 1707, the first fruits of the Tranquebar Mission.

From morning to night the missionaries were fully occupied. Ziegenbalg gave a good deal of time to the study of Tamil, and commenced a copious Tamil dictionary which occupied him several years, and was of great use to his successors in the mission. The language of conversation was studied as well as that of classical authors. The instruction of convicts and religious exercises formed other parts of the duties of the day.

The missionaries proposed to build a church for the use of the converts. The announcement was generally treated with ridicule by the European residents, but a few contributed something towards the building. The missionaries themselves gave more than a year's salary. It was built of stone, and opened 13 months after their first landing in India. The following month 9 adults were baptized. The missionaries preached every Sunday and Friday both in Tamil and Portuguese; school children were also publicly catechised.

In the year 1708 Ziegenbalg began to travel beyond the boundaries of the Tranquebar territory, that he might publish the Gospel more widely. In October of this year, also, he began to translate the New Testament into Tamil. The Dutch had a settlement at Negapatam, not far from Tranquebar, the governor of which was friendly to Missions. He invited the most learned Brahmans to meet Ziegenbalg; and a religious conference was held which lasted 5 hours.

The following year the missionaries were reduced to great distress. Two ships in which money had been remitted to them from Denmark were lost; the gifts of their friends in Germany were all expended in the maintenance of schools and teachers; and notwithstanding their frugal way of living, they must have suffered from absolute want, had not some persons in the town offered to lend them a little money. To add to their troubles, the governor, not only withheld from them the salary allowed them by the king, but threw Ziegenbalg into prison on a frivolous false charge.

Ziegenbalg quietly submitted, endeavouring to follow the example of his Saviour, who, "when He was reviled reviled not again." After four months' confinement, he was released.

In 1709 the missionaries received the much needed supplies of money from Denmark, with which also came a letter to the governor, enjoining him to assist and encourage the missionaries to the utmost of his power. The governor could no longer openly oppose the missionaries, who, above all, were cheered by the arrival of three fellow-labourers.

About this time also interest began to be awakened in the Tranquebar mission in England. The letters of Ziegenbalg and Plutschau came under the notice of a learned Danish clergyman, who was chaplain to the husband of Queen Anne. He translated them into English, and made them known to the Society for Promoting Christian Knowledge. It was resolved by the Society, that all possible assistance should be given to the translation of the Scriptures into the languages of India, and to the establishment of Christian schools. A letter was sent to Ziegenbalg, with a present of books and money for the mission. With a portion of the money received from England, Ziegenbalg purchased a garden at Porreiar, not far from Tranquebar, and erected a small house. Porreiar is now an important mission station.

The missionaries had as yet no printing press. They employed people to multiply copies of the works they had translated or composed by writing them on palm leaves, and circulating them among the people. Ziegenbalg wrote an earnest affictionate letter to Hindus, entreating them to worship the one true God, and to take refuge in the Saviour whom He has graciously provided. Copies of this letter and a Tamil translation of St. Matthew's Gospel were distributed by Ziegenbalg on his way to Madras. This visit led to the establishment of a mission school in that city.

The Tamil translation of the New Testament was completed

in May, 1711, but it could not be printed till 1714 through Tamil type sent out from Germany. Smaller type was afterwards cut at Tranquebar, and the manufacture of paper was attempted with good success.

Failing health obliged Plutschau to return to Europe in 1712. He could report that upwards of 200 converts had been baptized. Among them was a noted Tamil poet, called Kanabadi, who wrote a History of the Saviour in verse, and other works which are still esteemed by Tamil Christians.

In 1714, Ziegenbalg found it necessary to return to Europe for a short time. He greatly desired to see the King of Denmark to get some hindrances to his work removed, and to confer with friends in Germany and England about the mission. The Danish governor was in great alarm lest his cruel treatment of Ziegenbalg should be represented to the king, but his mind was set at rest on this point. Ziegenbalg took with him an intelligent Tamil convert who assisted him during the long voyage home in translating the Old Testament. He also began a Tamil grammar in Latin, and made additions to his dictionary.

Although the king of Denmark was then engaged in war, Ziegenbalg was very kindly received by him, and after the interview was sent home in a royal carriage. During his stay at home, his Tamil Grammar and Dictionary were printed at Halle, in Germany.

In England Ziegenbalg was welcomed with much affection and respect. The Christian Knowledge Society made him a liberal present of money, books, and paper; he was presented to the King George I., and the East India Company gave him a free passage to India. During the voyage out, Ziegenbalg proceeded with his translation of the Old Testament.

On landing at Madras in August 1716, he took measures with friends there to establish additional schools both in Danish and English territory. At Tranquebar, Ziegenbalg had a warm welcome, and soon after a seminary was established for the training of teachers and catechists. A new church was also erected as the old one was too small.

Early in 1717 the missionaries addressed letters to George I., giving him an account of the present state of the mission. The King replied in a Latin letter, of which the following is a translation:—

"Reverend and Beloved,—

"Your letters, dated the 20th January of the present year, were most welcome to us; not only because the work undertaken by you, of converting the heathen to the Christian faith, doth by the grace of God, prosper, but also because that in this our kingdom such a laudable zeal for the promotion of the Gospel prevails. We pray you may be endued with health and strength of body, that you may long continue to fulfil your ministry with good success; of which as we shall be rejoiced to hear, so you will always find us ready to succour you in whatever may tend to promote your work and to excite your zeal. We assure you of the continuance of our royal favour.

"Given at our Palace of Hampton Court, the 23rd August, A.D. 1717, in the 4th year of our reign.

"GEORGE R."

A most friendly and eloquent Latin letter was also addressed to the missionaries by the Archbishop of Canterbury.

Worn out with excessive toil, Ziegenbalg's strength was exhausted before he had completed his 36th year. On the morning of the 23rd February, 1719, he was seized with the pains of death. The friends who stood around his bed repeated some of the words of the Apostle Paul, "I have a desire to depart and to be with Christ." "That," said the dying man, "is what I long for. Washed from my sins in His blood, and clothed with His righteousness, may He bring me into His Kingdom." A number of Native Christians and school children stood in the verandahs. He desired that all would sing his favourite hymn, "Jesus, my refuge;" and when it was ended he calmly gave up his soul to God. His loss was mourned over by 355 converts, besides a large number under instruction.

A few months later three new missionaries from Europe came to Tranquebar. One of them, named Schultze, an able scholar and good man, completed Ziegenbalg's translation of the Old Testament, and translated the whole Bible into Hindustani. He established a mission in Madras. An English Church already existed there, built in 1680, about 60 years after its occupation by the East India Company. When in 1742 Schultze returned to his native land, the Native Christian congregation in Madras amounted to about 700 persons.

In 1726 the converts numbered 678; in 1736 they had increased to 2329; and during the next 10 years 3812 persons were baptized.

C. F. Schwartz.

One of the most useful missionaries that ever came to India was Christian Frederic Schwartz. He was born in Prussia in 1726. His mother, a pious woman, died while he was very young, but in her last moments she charged her husband to train up the child in remembrance that he had been dedicated to God's service. In his 16th year, he was sent to a school that he might be prepared for the University. His father, though a man of some wealth, gave his son only as much money as was required for his necessary expenses. He thus escaped many snares which proved fatal to others. Twice when attacked by dangerous illness, he resolved, should his life be spared, to devote himself to the service of his Maker; but with returning health his good resolutions were forgotten. Yet the prayers of his mother had gone up for a memorial before God, and after a time he accepted Jesus Christ as his Saviour, and continued His faithful follower till the end of his life.

In 1746 Schwartz, proceeded to Halle to study at the University, then distinguished for the Christian character of its professors. Here he made the acquaintance of Schultze, who had been for more than 20 years a missionary in South India. Schultze recommended him to learn Tamil, that he might assist in carrying through the press a new edition of the Bible which was to be printed at Halle. So high an opinion was formed of Schwartz, that he was encouraged to offer himself as a missionary to India. He agreed to do so if his father's consent could be obtained. Although Frederic was the eldest son, the father, after long consideration and earnest prayer, laying his hand on the head of his son, solemnly gave him his blessing, charged him to forget his country and his father's house, and to go forth amongst the heathen to win souls unto Christ.

Frederic then gave up his share of his father's inheritance to his brothers and sisters, and hastened back to Halle to prepare for his departure. After visiting Denmark, he went to England for a few weeks, during which he applied himself to the study of English. He met with a kind reception in England, and was granted a free passage to India by the East India Company, where he arrived in July, 1750.

Schwartz landed at Cuddalore, from which, after a short stay, he proceeded to Tranquebar. He applied himself with great diligence to the study of Tamil, and made such rapid progress that in less than 4 months from his landing in India he preached his first sermon. Through teaching in the Tamil School and by conversing freely with all he met, whether Christians or Hindus, he gradually acquired readiness in the use of the language.

One of the duties assigned to Schwartz was the preparation of adult candidates for baptism. He took the utmost care to ascertain, not only the religious knowledge, but the Christian disposition of those under instruction. In the case of persons from a distance, baptism was often deferred for several months, that the missionaries might become better acquainted with their character and previous conduct. In 1751, four hundred persons were added by baptism to the Tamil congregation.

Schwartz, for several years, studied the sacred writings of the Hindus. This enabled him at any time to command the attention of the people by allusions to their favourite books.

The elder missionaries at Tranquebar seeing the talents and zeal of Schwartz, committed to his superintendence the various congregations and schools south of the Cauvery. From the time that he rose in the morning till he retired to rest at night, he was constantly employed.

On the 19th July, 1756, the fiftieth anniversary of the landing of Ziegenbalg and Plutschau was celebrated. During the half century the Mission had passed through many changes and trials, but 11,000 souls had been added to the Church.

In 1760 Schwartz was invited to visit Ceylon, where he spent three months. His labours were most useful to the Christian population of the places which he visited. Before leaving for India, he went to Point Pedro, in the north of the island, to see the great tree under which Baldæus, an eminent Missionary, had been wont to preach one hundred years before. The concluding entry in the journal of his visit to Ceylon is a humble prayer that God, for Christ's sake, would pardon all his sins of omission and commission—duties he had left undone, and wrong things he had done, and that a lasting blessing might rest on all his labours which were agreeable to the Divine Word.

For several years Schwartz had regarded Tranquebar as his home, but Tanjore and Trichinopoly afterwards became the principal sphere of his labours. In 1762, accompanied by one of his colleagues, went on foot to Tanjore and Trichinopoly, preaching as usual, by the way, to both Christians and Hindus. At Tanjore, Schwartz was permitted to speak freely about the Christian religion even within the Raja's palace; and the prince, hearing, from one of his chief officers, of the missionary and his words, desired that he might be invited to repeat his visit. The Raja himself was present when he came again to the palace, and, though concealed by a screen, heard all that passed.

From Tanjore Schwartz proceeded to Trichinopoly, then as now a large military station. He then became known to Mahomed Ali, Nawab of the Carnatic. He was walking in the gardens of the palace one day, when the Nawab happened to be there. The prince perceiving him, sat down, desired the missionary to approach, and offered him some refreshment, which, however he declined. A few days afterwards the Nawab met him again, and entered into friendly conversation.

To qualify himself for more extensive usefulness, Schwartz for some time applied himself diligently to the study of Persian and Hindustani. The former was the language of the Muhammadan Court, and the latter was in use among Muhammadans throughout India.

During the siege of Madura in 1763 and 1764 by the British troops and the forces of the Nawab, Schwartz went there for a time to minister to the sick and wounded as well as conduct Divine service. When the city fell, Schwartz received as a present 600 pagodas which he gave for the benefit of the Tamil congregation and school.

In 1766 he became missionary at Trichinopoly of the Christian Knowledge Society. He was now 40 years of age. A gentleman thus describes his appearance and mode of life at that time:

"Figure to yourself a stout, well-made man, somewhat above the middle height, erect in his carriage and address, with a complexion rather dark though healthy, black curled hair, and a

C. F. SCHWARTZ.

manly and engaging countenance, expressive of unaffected candour, ingenuousness and benevolence; and you will have an idea of what Mr. Schwartz appeared to be at first sight. He had much to do with very narrow means. His whole income was *ten pagodas per month,* or about 48 *l* per annum. He obtained of the commanding officer a room in an old Hindu building which was just large enough to hold his bed and himself, and in which few men could stand upright. A dish of rice and vegetables, dressed after the manner of the natives, was what he could always cheerfully sit down to, and a piece of dimity (cotton cloth) dyed black, and other materials of the same homely sort, sufficed him for an annual supply of clothing."

At Trichinopoly Schwartz found a large English garrison without a Chaplain. He prevailed upon the soldiers to meet in a large apartment in an old native building; but in time they subscribed money to build a large and handsome church.

In 1767, war with Hyder Ali, Sultan of Mysore, broke out, which continued for two years. At one time, the arms of Hyder were so successful, that it was feared that Trichinopoly would fall into his power, but three days' heavy rain obliged him to withdraw his troops. Schwartz devoted himself with much zeal and sympathy to the care of the sick and wounded.

When peace was restored in 1769, Schwartz visited Tanjore, where he spent 3 weeks in preaching and examining the schools. He was then introduced to Tuljaji, the Raja, with whom he had a long conversation on the subject of religion. Sweetmeats were afterwards brought in. When Schwartz had eaten a little he said, "We Christians are accustomed to give thanks when we partake of food, and to pray that the strength which we derive from it may be employed in the service of God the giver." With the Raja's approval, he offered up a short prayer. The Raja had heard that Christians sang songs of praise to God, so he asked Schwartz to sing a hymn. He complied by singing a few verses of the hymn, "My God, to Thee this heart I bring," which begins by acknowledging the soul's guilt, ignorance, and poverty, and ends with entire surrender to God. The Raja expressed his satisfaction, saying that he had never before heard the like from any European.

Some time after this, the Raja wished to send Schwartz on a political mission to Madras. He said to Schwartz, 'Padre, I have confidence in you, because you are indifferent to money." Although Schwartz was willing to help the Raja, his ministers were so deceitful that he was obliged to decline the mission.

In 1779 Schwartz was requested to go to Madras, where the Governor, Sir Thomas Rumbold, wished to speak with him. To his surprise the Governor told him that Hyder Ali was supposed to meditate war, and Schwartz was asked to go to his capital to assure him that the English entertained peaceable thoughts. Schwartz was selected for the Mission, because he understood Hindustani, and could speak to Hyder without an interpreter. Another reason was that he would not be bribed. The Mission involved some danger, but in the hope of averting war, Schwartz undertook the journey, receiving no more than his travelling expenses. Hyder received him kindly and bade him sit next to himself, without requiring him to take of his shoes. He was told that he might stay in Seringapatam as long as he pleased; but after receiving a letter which he was to deliver to the Governor of

Madras, he took his leave of Hyder. On entering his palanquin Schwartz found Rs. 300 which Hyder had sent him to defray the expenses of his journey. Schwartz would have returned the money, but this would have been an insult. It was given to an orphan school.

The following year Hyder, professing not to believe the desire for peace expressed by the Madras Government, invaded the Carnatic, with an army of nearly a lakh of men, desolating the country like locusts. During the next three years, multitudes perished by the sword, famine, and pestilence. Schwartz foreseeing war, laid in a large stock of rice when it was cheap, which was of the greatest benefit to the Native Christians and orphans. Numbers had fled to Tanjore for refuge, so that the stock of provisions was exhausted, and many perished from hunger. Formerly when the country people brought provisions, they were defrauded by the Raja's officers, so they refused to bring more in spite of the entreaties of the Raja and his minister. The Raja then applied to Schwartz. He sent out letters in every direction asking for supplies, and promising to pay for them with his own hands. In a short time 80,000 measures of rice were brought into the fort. Schwartz paid the people, and sent them home quite satisfied.

Hyder, in the midst of the war, ordered his officers not to molest "the venerable padre; for he is a holy man." In the third year of the war Hyder died, and was succeeded by his son Tippu, who was obliged to sue for peace.

The Raja of Tanjore, suffering from an incurable disease, had abandoned the management of his kingdom to a minister who was a cruel extortioner. The people after appealing in vain to the Raja for redress, fled in crowds to the adjacent countries. Large tracts lay waste for want of labourers to cultivate them. The Raja tried to win them back, but they distrusted his promises, and refused to come. He then asked Mr. Schwartz to write to him, and such was their confidence in him that 7,000 came back in one day.

At Tanjore, notwithstanding his numerous duties, Schwartz sometimes gave religious instruction to the sons of European gentlemen resident near Tanjore. One of his pupils was Sir Alexander Johnston, who became Chief Justice of Ceylon. He thus gives his recollections of Schwartz: "I well remember his peculiarly venerable appearance, the tall and erect figure, the head white with years, the features on which I loved to look, the mingled dignity and amenity of his demeanour."

As was often the case with Indian Rajas on account of their immoral lives, Tuljagi had no son of his own to succeed him. He therefore adopted the son of a cousin, a boy ten years old, whom he named Serfoji Raja. Shortly before his death, he sent for Schwartz to entreat him to become guardian of young Serfoji. Pointing to the child he said, "This is not my son, but yours; into your hand I deliver him." Schwartz could not undertake such a charge, but during the remainder of his life he acted like a father to the youth, and did all he could for his benefit.

Towards the close of 1797, Schwartz was attacked by a severe illness, and it became evident that his end was near. No longer able to hold service in the Church, he caused the Native Christians to come to his house, where he expounded the Scriptures and prayed with them in Tamil, as he had been used to do. The children also came daily to him to read the Bible, and sing their hymns.

Shortly before his death, when hymns were sung, he revived and tried to sing with them. Among his last words were the following: "Oh Lord, hitherto Thou hast preserved me; hitherto Thou hast brought me; and hast bestowed innumerable benefits upon me. Do what is pleasing in Thy sight. I commend my spirit into Thy hands; cleanse and adorn it with the righteousness of my Redeemer, and receive me into the arms of Thy mercy." Soon after he bowed his head, and peacefully departed to his Master's rest.

Serfoji wrote the following inscription which was placed upon the tomb of Schwartz:

"Firm wast thou, humble and wise,
Honest, pure, free from disguise;
Father of orphans, the widow's support,
Comfort in sorrow of every sort.
To the benighted, dispenser of light,
Doing, and pointing to, that which is right,
Blessing to princes, to people, to me;
May I, my father, be worthy of thee;
Wisheth and prayeth thy Saraboji."

PROTESTANT MISSIONS ACCORDING TO NATIONALITIES.

Some account will now be given of the efforts to make known the Gospel among the principal nations of India. About a hundred languages and dialects are spoken. Space permits only the most important to be noticed, and even in their case only a few leading events can be mentioned.

BENGALIS.

Bengali, next to Hindi, is the language spoken by the greatest number in India. The Bengalis amount to nearly 42 millions: one in every 7 of the inhabitants of India is a Bengali.

Bengal formed one of the 5 outlying kingdoms of Aryan India. It includes the lower courses of the Ganges and Brahmaputra, and is chiefly a large rice-producing plain. The numerous rivers yield a plentiful supply of fish, which forms an important article of food.

In some parts every house has its canoe, as the country is under water during the rainy season. Some of the canoes are so small that a man can carry one on his head; others are larger, and have a covering.

Language.—Bengali belongs to the northern family of languages. The character is the same as the Nagri, but rounded for greater facility in writing. There is a fondness for the sound *o*: thus Manu becomes Monu. In point of numbers speaking of Bengali ranks next to Hindi.

BENGALI.

কেননা ঈশ্বর জগতের প্রতি এমত প্রেম করিলেন, যে আপনার অদ্বিতীয় পুত্রকে দান করিলেন; যেন তাঁহাতে বিশ্বাসকারি প্রত্যেক জন বিনষ্ট না হইয়া অনন্ত জীবন পায়।

Muhammadans mix with Bengali a number of Arabic and Persian words. Their language is called Musalman-Bengali.

Though small and weak in appearance, the Bengalis can endure a considerable amount of fatigue: "In active pursuits," says Beverly, "the Bengali is timid and slothful; but in intellect he is subtle and sharpwitted." A Bengali journalist thus points out a prominent defect: "One of our national poets describing the character of a certain individual, says,—'*He was mountain-*

BENGALI CHRISTIANS.

like in words, in deeds mustard-seed-like.' It is not too much to say that, in these words is comprehended the predominant feature of our national character."

It is estimated that of the Hindus in Bengal about three-fourths are worshippers of the wife of Siva, under the names of Durga and Kali. She is represented as a black woman with four hands, wearing a necklace of skulls, and dancing on the body of Siva. Elated by her victory over the demon who attacked her in the form of a buffalo, she danced so furiously that the earth trembled beneath her weight. As she did not stop when asked, Siva lay down among the slain. She stopped when she caught sight of her husband. The *Durga Puja*, the chief festival in Bengal, is intended to celebrate this victory.

The Bengalis have passed through different phases. Forty years ago, they were the leaders in social and other reforms: Under the influence of false patriotism, there is now a re-actionary movement among some. Everything Indian is right, because it is Indian; that anything is foreign is regarded as a sufficient condemnation. Intelligent men see the folly of this. *The Indian Messenger* has the following remarks on such re-actionaries :—

"It is easy to convince an ignorant man. It is not very difficult to dispel the erroneous views of a superstitious man. But your educated re-actionary is the strangest creature living and the most difficult to deal with. Persistent advocacy of wrong, shutting the eyes to the rays of knowledge growing brighter every day, efforts to make the worse appear the better reason, end in moral shipwreck." September 27, 1891.

Some of the most distinguished Indians in modern times have been Bengalis. Among them may be specially mentioned Rammohun Roy and Keshub Chunder Sen, the greatest Indian religious reformers of the century.

Early Missions.

First Protestant Missionary.—The first Protestant Missionary to Bengal was John Daniel Kiernander, of the Danish Mission at Cuddalore. During the war between the French and the English in the Carnatic, mission work there was stopped. Kiernander, therefore, resolved to open new ground, and in 1758 went to Calcutta, a year after the battle of Plassey. His first step was to open a school, the pupils in which at the end of a year had increased to 135. Kiernander also went about preaching, and a Native congregation was gradually formed. He married a wife, with a large income, of which a considerable portion was devoted to the use of the Mssion. He built in Calcutta what is now called the "Old Mission Church," at a cost of half a lakh of rupees, nearly the whole of it from his own resources. In the ten years ending in 1776, there were 495 persons added to the Mission. Kiernander laboured on till old age, though pecuniary troubles, caused by the extravagance of his son, beclouded the closing years of his life.

State of English Society.—Last century there were few English ladies in Calcutta. Many Europeans kept native women; some, like Muhammadans, had several. There was a great deal of drunkenness. Sundays were spent in shooting, gambling, horse racing, &c. Some Europeans sought to please their Hindu concubines by worshipping their favourite idols.

There were, however, a few good men. Among them were Charles Grant, who came out to India with his wife and her sister, and rose to a high position in the Civil Service. William Chambers, Master of Chancery in the Supreme Court of Calcutta, who had been influenced by Schwartz, and who had married Grant's sister-in-law; and George Udny, another Civilian. While the great majority of Europeans were opposed to Christian Missions which condemned their immoral lives, the three mentioned above were their warm supporters. To them should be added the Rev. David Brown, who came out to India, as Chaplain of the European Asylum for orphan children. He took so much interest in Missions, that he gave up his salary as Chaplain rather than discontinue his services at Kiernander's Church. One of his sons was Mr. C. P. Brown, a Madras Civilian distinguished as a Telugu scholar. These good men made several attempts to establish Missions in India, but for a time they were unsuccessful.

Serampore Mission.—William Carey was born in England in 1761 of poor parents. When 14 years of age he tried to work as a field labourer; but as he could not stand exposure to the sun, in his 17th year he became a shoemaker. As a boy he had learned by heart a Latin Vocabulary. Meeting with a book containing some Greek words, he began to study that language. Up till this time, Carey had been careless about religion. He now felt that he had been sinful, and needed a change of heart. At first he tried to quiet his conscience by attention to the outward forms of religion, and sought to be saved through his own merits; but when he gained more knowledge, he felt that he could not atone for his past sins, nor work out a righteousness of his own. He joyfully accepted the Lord Jesus Christ as his Saviour, and sought the help of the Holy Spirit to enable him to overcome sin. Not long afterwards Carey was invited to preach in a village, where there were no religious services. This he did Sabbath after Sabbath, and afterwards he was appointed to the ministry.

Carey imprudently married early and had great difficulty in supporting his family. Besides working during the day as a shoemaker, he opened an evening school. Amid all his hardships, he laboured diligently to acquire knowledge. He never sat at work without a book before him.

Accounts of the ignorance and superstition of many nations, led Carey to form a map to show the different religions of the world, which he employed in teaching geography. The last command of the Lord Jesus Christ to His disciples was, "Go and teach all nations." For some years this was obeyed, and great numbers embraced Christianity. Last century it was almost entirely forgotten. At a meeting of ministers in 1791, Carey urged the duty of forming a society to spread the Gospel in heathen lands. This was not then agreed to, but he was asked to publish a pamphlet he had written on the subject. The following year he preached a sermon, the two divisions of which were: "EXPECT GREAT THINGS FROM GOD;" "ATTEMPT GREAT THINGS FOR GOD." Four months later, in October, 1792, it was resolved to form the Baptist Missionary Society,* and Carey offered to become its first missionary.

At that time no one could go out to India in an English ship without a license. If they did so, they would be sent back immediately. Carey obtained a passage in a ship belonging to the king of Denmark. At first he tried to support himself, while he also worked as a missionary. After acquiring a good knowledge of Bengali, he began the study of Sanskrit, and read a great part of the Mahabharata.

The East India Company was then strongly opposed to missionaries coming to India as it was feared that their preaching would create a rebellion. As 4 missionaries were coming out to join Carey, it was agreed that they should all settle at Serampore, a small Danish settlement, 13 miles north of Calcutta. Two of the 4 missionaries died soon; the other two lived for many years. One was William Ward, a printer, the other was Joshua Marshman. The three missionaries agreed to live together, and to throw all their earnings into a common stock. They were to live economically and spend all they could on schools and printing the Scriptures. Ward was a good printer, and the press which he established earned several thousand rupees a year. Mr. and Mrs. Marshman set up two boarding schools, which soon yielded Rs. 800 a month. Carey was appointed a teacher in the College of Fort William and Bengali Translator to Government, receiving in all Rs. 1,250 a month. From that he retained only Rs. 50 a month for his private expenses; Mr. Marshman took Rs. 30, and Mr. Ward Rs. 20. Carey took rather more on account of his duties at the College and appearance at Government House.

With the earnings of the Serampore Missionaries and some help from England, Mission Stations were opened in different parts of the country. Krishna Chundra Pal, the first convert, was baptized in 1802. He composed a hymn, a translation of which is still sometimes sung. The first verse is as follows:

O Thou, my soul, forget no more
The Friend who all thy misery bore;
Let every idol be forgot,
But, O my soul, forget him not.

* The Baptists are a body of Christians so called from their opinions about baptism.

WILLIAM CAREY.

In 1810 there were 300 converts, of whom 105 had been added that year.

Carey's first important work was the translation of the Bible into Bengali, and for 40 years he was engaged either in translating himself or in revising translations made by others. He and his companions formed the grand design of translating the Scriptures into all the languages of the East. For this they had several advantages. Carey had a great aptitude for acquiring languages. The assistance of learned pandits connected with the College of Fort William could be obtained; the missionaries had one of the best libraries in India, a large printing establishment, and a letter foundry able to produce types in the different languages.

With the assistance of pandits, Carey himself prepared the Bengali, Hindi, Marathi, and Sanskrit translations. In other cases pandits from different parts of India translated from the Sanskrit with their own vernaculars, Carey and his associates reading the versions before they were printed. Marshman undertook the Chinese. The whole Bible was printed in Bengali, Oriya, Assamese, Hindi, and Marathi; the New Testament in 22 languages, and Gospels in some others. Under the circumstances the translations were imperfect; but they were useful in their day, and helped to prepare the way for others more accurate. Besides translating the Scriptures, Carey prepared Grammars in several languages, and a Bengali Dictionary.

The earliest movement against widow burning was made by the Serampore missionaries; the Agricultural and Horticultural Society for India was founded through Carey; and he sought to establish the system of savings banks to counteract the tendency to get into debt; the first Bengali newspaper was commenced at Serampore.

In 1818 the Serampore missionaries proposed the establishment of a College for instruction in "Eastern literature and European Science." It was to include the study of Sanskrit, Arabic, and English; the preparation of manuals of science, the training of teachers, and a theological institute for Christian students. Although Dr. Duff has the honour of giving a great impulse to English education all over India, Carey and his associates felt its importance several years before he came to the country.

The College, for a number of years, was largely attended and very useful. The establishment of Mission Colleges in Calcutta, more convenient to students than Serampore, led to the giving up of the College Department in 1879, but a Training Institution for Christian Mission Agents is still carried on.

Carey laboured till the last. When he could no longer sit at his desk, he corrected proof sheets when lying on his couch. On the morning of June 9th, 1834, he passed away to his reward in his 73rd year.

Although he had been in labours most abundant and highly honoured, he never lost his humility. "Let my funeral," said he, "be as plain as may be. Let these words be put on my tombstone:—

"William Carey, born August 17th, 1761, and died—
A wretched, poor, and helpless worm,
On Thy kind arms, I fall."

English Chaplains and Bishops.

Chaplains are ministers sent out for Europeans; but some of them, while attending diligently to their immediate duties, took a warm interest in missions. The labours of the Rev. David Brown have already been noticed. Dr. Claudius Buchanan was a man of similar spirit. He encouraged the Serampore Missionaries in their translations, giving himself Rs. 5,000 in aid of their work; he travelled to the southern extremity of India that he might assist in providing the Syrian Churches with the Scriptures; and he offered prizes to the British Universities to excite an interest in India among the students.

Thomason was another chaplain of like character. The most distinguished of them was Henry Martyn, but as he laboured in North India, he will be noticed under that head.

India opened to Missionaries in 1813.—The East India Company, in its early days, rather favoured Missions; but a change took place in its servants in India, many of whom were bitterly opposed to the preaching of the Gospel. As already mentioned, Carey and his companions had to seek shelter under the Danish flag at Serampore; some missionaries were not allowed even to land. These despotic proceedings, contrary to the principles of religious liberty, gave great offence to good men in England. When the Charter of the East India Company was renewed in 1793, Wilberforce tried to secure a clause stating that "It is the peculiar and bounden duty of the British Legislature to promote by all just and prudent means the interest and happiness of the inhabitants of the British dominions in India; and that for these ends such measures ought to be adopted as may gradually tend to their advancement in useful knowledge, and to their religious and moral improvement." The India House raised such an alarm that the clause was thrown out, and for 20 years the Company had the power of excluding missionaries.

When the East India Company's Charter was renewed in 1813, Wilberforce and his friends, in spite of great opposition, secured the insertion of a clause that, "it was the duty of this country to promote the introduction of useful knowledge and of religious and moral improvement in India, and that facilities be afforded by law to persons desirous of going to and remaining in India to accomplish these benevolent designs." The Charter also provided for the establishment of an Indian bishopric, and required a sum of not less than a lakh of rupees to be set apart each year for the improvement of literature and promotion of a knowledge of science.

First Indian Bishops.—In 1814, Thomas Fanshaw Middleton, a distinguished Greek scholar and good man, was appointed the first English Bishop of Calcutta. One of his earliest efforts was to increase the supply of good books through the Christian Knowledge Society. He encouraged the establishment of schools, and was very friendly to the study of English, which he hoped would lead the people of India to *think*. He made several long journeys, seeking both to benefit Europeans and to encourage Missions. Among other places he visited Tanjore, where the Raja presented to him a portrait of Schwartz.

The object which Bishop Middleton chiefly set before himself was the establishment of a college to train Indian Christians as preachers and teachers, to give a good English education to Hindus and Muhammadans, to translate the Scriptures and prepare other Christian and useful literature; and to receive English missionaries on their first arrival in India. The foundation stone of a noble building on the banks of the Hughli, to the south of Calcutta, was laid by the Bishop in December, 1820; but several years elapsed before it was completed. The first principal was the Rev. W. H. Mill, a learned and good man. Bishop Middleton was not spared to watch long over the institution which he founded. In July, 1822, he gently breathed his last.

Although there were some able and earnest men connected with Bishop's College, the grand designs of its founder were not fulfilled. Like Serampore College, its situation was inconvenient for students. In 1878, at the request of Bishop Johnson, the building was sold to Government for an Engineering College. In 1880

BISHOP HEBER.

the college was reopened in Calcutta, where, under the Rev. H. Whitehead, its usefulness has been revived.

In 1823 Reginald Heber was appointed Bishop Middleton's successor. At Oxford he had been the most distinguished student of his time. His prize poem, "Palestine," entitled him to a place among English poets. Some years afterwards he wrote the well-known missionary hymn, beginning as follows:

"From Greenland's icy mountains,
From India's coral strand,
Where Africa's sunny fountains
Roll down their golden sand,

From many an ancient river,
From many a palmy plain,
They call us to deliver
Their land from error's chain."

Besides being an accomplished scholar, Heber was remarkable for his winning manners, his unselfishness, and desire to do good. During the long voyage to India, besides seeking to benefit all on board the ship, he studied carefully both Hindustani and Persian. The greater part of Bishop Heber's short Indian career was spent in visiting his large diocese. His *Indian Journal* gives an excellent account of the state of the country at that time. During his second tour he died suddenly at Trichinopoly in 1826, only about two years after his arrival in India.

Among Heber's successors, may be specially mentioned Bishop Wilson, who built the Calcutta Cathedral and had a long episcopate, and Bishop Cotton, imbued with the spirit of Dr. Arnold, who was accidentally drowned in the Gorai river.

MISSIONS NOW AT WORK.

Baptist Mission.—The work commenced by the Serampore Mission was continued by the Baptist Missionary Society, and gradually extended. The Rev. Dr. Yates greatly improved the Bengali translation of the Bible, and the Rev. Dr. Wenger, in addition to Bengali revision, did much for the Sanskrit version. The Baptist Mission Press, established in Calcutta, has printed, besides the Scriptures and other Christian literature, the numerous oriental publications of the Bengal Asiatic Society.

Several mofussil stations are occupied. One of the largest missions is in the Backergunge district, separated from Jessore by one of the chief mouths of the Ganges. The Serampore Missionaries established a school at Barisal, the chief station, in 1823, in which instruction was imparted in English. From this small beginning a prosperous and extensive mission has gradually sprung up. There is a promising mission at Dacca, the capital of Eastern Bengal. At Serampore there are Theological and Normal Classes.

In 1893 there were connected with the Baptist Mission 35 missionaries, 3,991 Church members, 11,056 Christians including church members, and 3,702 children at school.

London Mission.—The London Missionary Society sent out the Rev. N. Forsyth, its first missionary to India in 1798. He settled at Chinsurah, a Dutch station, 20 miles north of Calcutta. He continued alone in the work till 1812, when he was joined by the Rev. R. May. Mr. May established a large number of vernacular schools, which received a liberal grant from Government. In 1849 the Chinsurah mission passed into the hands of the Free Church of Scotland. In 1816 the Rev. Messrs. Townley and Keith were sent out to begin a mission in Calcutta. In 1826 work was commenced among

DR. MULLENS.

the villages to the south of Calcutta. The Rev. A. F. Lacroix laboured among them and in Calcutta for many years.

In 1837 an Educational Institution was established at Bhowanipore, a suburb of Calcutta. Chiefly through the efforts of the Rev. T. Boaz, a noble building was erected for it in 1853. The Rev. Dr. Mullens, afterwards Secretary of the London Missionary Society, had charge of it for a time. He wrote a valuable prize essay on *Vedantism, Brahmism, and Christianity.* Mrs. Mullens, a daughter of the Rev. Mr. Lacroix, was a zealous worker in the cause of female education. She also wrote *Phulmani and Karuna,** describing the faults and virtues of Indian Christians, and fitted to do much good. It has been translated into the principal languages of India.

Berhampore, in the district of Murshidabad, 180 miles north of Calcutta, is the other mission centre in Bengal. The mission was begun in 1824. Evangelistic work is carried on in some villages around.

In 1894 there were connected with the London Mission, 9 English missionaries, 473 church members, 1757 adherents, and 3875 children at school.

Church Mission.—A Corresponding Committee in connection with the Church Missionary Society was formed in Calcutta in 1812, but it was not until 1815 that a mission was planted in Calcutta. This was at Kidderpore, in the suburbs, where a site for a school had been given by a Brahman. The first two missionaries sent out to Bengal were the Rev. Messrs. Greenwood and Schroeter, who reached Calcutta in 1816. The following year a commencement was made at Burdwan. Here the Rev. J. J. Weitbrecht laboured for many years. In 1821 the Society established its headquarters in Mirzapore, near the centre of Calcutta; schools were opened, and a printing press was commenced. The most important Mission of the Society was commenced in 1831, at Krishnagar, in the district of Nadiya, noted for its Sanskrit Schools. The Rev. W. J. Deer was one of the earliest missionaries. Numerous schools were planted throughout the district, and the Gospel was preached from village to village. About 1838, within a few months, 3,000 persons, on the east side of the river Jellinghi, came forward to embrace Christianity. The motive in most cases was the hope of temporal help. They had suffered from a famine, and they expected the mission to supply them with seed-corn and other necessaries. For a considerable time they were unsatisfactory; but through patient teaching they gradually improved. There is now a band of "Associated Evangelists," young Englishmen, with Indian helpers, moving from village to village. Krishnagar has a Normal School for the training of teachers; in Calcutta there is a Divinity School.

---

* English edition sold by Mr. A. T. Scott, Tract Depôt, Madras, Price 2 As.

In 1893 the Society had 7 English ordained Missionaries labouring among Bengalis, 6581 Native Christians, 1254 communicants, and 4157 children at School.

Gospel Society.—The Calcutta Diocesan Committee of this Society was formed in 1825 at a public meeting at which Bishop Heber presided. Bishop's College, founded by Bishop Middleton, was early placed under its agents. They also superintended several schools made over to them by the Christian Knowledge Society in 1828. The Rev. W. Morton, who was the first missionary sent by the Society to Bengal, reached Chinsurah in 1829. Tallyganj, near Calcutta, was occupied the same year. In 1833 other villages, as Barripore, Jangira, &c., were taken up.

In 1893 there were 8 Missionaries, 4280 baptized persons, 1797 communicants, and 1253 pupils in school, connected with the S. P. G. Society in Bengal.

Scottish Missions.—It has been mentioned that English was taught in the Serampore College established in 1818; but it received its great impulse from Dr. Duff, of whom a short account will now be given.

The Rev. Alexander Duff was sent out by the Church of Scotland as its first missionary to India. He left England in October, 1829, and after nearly an 8 months' voyage, during which he was twice shipwrecked, reached Calcutta at the end of May, 1830. His special work was to establish a Missionary College. At that time Sanskrit, Persian, and Arabic were taught in Government Colleges, and even many Englishmen in high position approved of such teaching in preference to English. Duff took an opposite view. He held that English was "the best and amplest channel for speedily letting in the full stream of European knowledge on the minds of those who were destined to influence and direct the national intellect and heart of India." In this Duff was encouraged by Rammohun Roy. The native languages were by no means to be neglected, but the English key to knowledge was to be given to India.

The institution was opened on July 12th, 1830. It commenced with 5 young men, but before the end of the first week there were more than 300 applicants. A simple yet thorough course of instruction in the English language in all the classes was laid down, and the institution soon achieved a wonderful popularity. At the end of the first year a public examination of the scholars was held in a spacious hall in Calcutta, and was attended by a large number of European gentlemen and ladies, besides some Indians of high rank. On the reopening of the seminary, the number of new applications for admission was more than trebled. Elementary teaching was gradually advanced to a collegiate course, somewhat similar to that pursued at one of the Scottish universities. In nine years the five

REV. DR. ALEXANDER DUFF.

who entered the Institution on the day of its commencement increased to an average attendance of 800.

Duff's views on English education were held by Macaulay, then Legal Member of the Governor-General's Council; and defended by him in an admirable Minute on education in India. They were adopted by Lord William Bentinck, the Governor-General, and a Resolution was passed in favour of English education, which gave a great impulse to it all over India. The effect, on the whole, has been highly beneficial. Sanskrit contains false history, false science, false philosophy, false religion. The more it is studied, the more errors are acquired. Pandits, whose knowledge is confined to Sanskrit, are "learned fools," the most bigoted portion of the people, the greatest opponents of reform. It is true that English contains some pernicious literature; but, on the whole, it has tended greatly to elevate India. More and more enlightened views on every point are gradually spreading.

A rural mission is maintained in the Hughli district, where several stations are occupied.

In 1893 the Free Church had in Bengal 7 ordained missionaries, 211 communicants, 298 baptised adherents, and 3474 pupils under instruction.

Church of Scotland.—In 1843, Dr. Duff and his fellow-missionaries left the Church of Scotland, and joined the Free Church. The old Institution in Cornwallis Square has since been maintained by the Church of Scotland, and has at present a large number of students.

In 1893 there were 5 ordained missionaries, 86 communicants, 85 baptised adherents, and 1708 scholars connected with the Church of Scotland Mission in Bengal.

Wesleyan Mission.—In 1829, the Rev. Messrs. P. Percival and T. Hodson were appointed to Calcutta. They preached, built a native chapel, and established schools; but after three or four years the station was abandoned, Mr. Percival being sent to Ceylon and Mr. Hodson to Mysore. In 1862 the mission was re-opened by the Rev. Messrs. Broadbent and Highfield, and the work has since been carried steadily forward. Several outstations have been occupied.

In 1893 there were 8 English missionaries, 451 church members, and 94 on trial, and 2657 children at school connected with the Mission.

American Methodist Episcopal Mission.—This mission has branches in nearly every province of India. Details are wanting: a general account of its work will be given under Hindi.

Oxford Mission.—This Mission, supported mainly by the *alumni* of Oxford University, was founded in 1880 under the charge of the Rev. E. J. Willis, with a view, more particularly, to work among the educated Hindus of Calcutta. Lectures are delivered and visits to the Mission house are invited. Some part in education is also undertaken. *The Epiphany*, for circulation among non-Christians, is issued weekly.

FEMALE EDUCATION.

This is noticed separately on account of its importance.

Occasionally in ancient India pandits taught their wives and daughters to read, as Pandita Rama Bai was taught Sanskrit in modern times; but such cases were very exceptional. The general feeling was that women did not require education, and, if obtained, would be used for improper purposes. No mantras or religious services were ordained for women; their husbands were to be regarded as their gods, and through them they would obtain admission to heaven. Female education in India originated with Christian Missions.

The Serampore Missionaries, at an early period, established several girls' schools, and through the efforts of Mr. Ward, Miss Cooke was sent out to India in 1821 to devote herself to female education. She learned the colloquial Bengali quickly, entered heartily into her work, and with such spirit that in the course of a few months, in connection with the Church Missionary Society, she had established 10 schools, containing 277 girls. She displayed great tact in her intercourse with Bengali ladies, and exercised a winning influence over both them and their children. These schools early received the aid and patronage of the Marchioness of Hastings, who, in her zeal, traversed the gullies and back streets of the city, in which some of them were situated, and thereby produced a great impression on all classes. In 1823 the schools had increased to 22, and the pupils to 400.

The following year, the Ladies' Society for Female Education in Calcutta was established, to which the schools were transferred. In 1826 they were 30 in number, with an attendance of 600 children. During the same year a Central School was erected, the foundation stone being laid by Lady Amherst, wife of the Governor-General. On this occasion many Indian gentlemen and ladies with their daughters were present. Among them was Raja Badinath Roy, who had contributed Rs. 20,000 to the undertaking.

Nearly all the Missionary Societies working in Calcutta have done more or less for female education. There are a few missions devoted to it exclusively.

Zenana Teaching.—The Rev. T. Smith of Calcutta, so long ago as 1840, proposed a scheme for the home education of women of the upper classes; but at the time it met with no practical response. In 1854 it was taken up by the Rev. J. Fordyce, with the cordial co-operation of Mr. Smith. Soon afterwards Mrs. Sale, Mrs. Mullens, and the Normal School Society entered the field, and the work spread in Calcutta.

In Calcutta and its environs in 1890 there were 1031 pupils in Female Boarding Schools, 7791 in Day Schools, and 2689 under instruction in Zenanas.

The Brahmo Samaj.

This movement may be noticed as an indirect result of Christian Missions and English education. Its founder, Rammohun Roy, first learned monotheism from the Bible and the Koran, and then tried to find it in the Upanishads. In 1820 he published, "The Precepts of Jesus, the Guide to Peace and Happiness; extracted from the books of the New Testament." As already mentioned, he aided Dr. Duff at the commencement of his work in Calcutta. Along with some friends he established a Society with weekly meetings for worship and the delivery of a sermon—before unknown among the Hindus. A building was purchased, and in 1830 the first Hindu Theistic Church was opened.

RAMMOHUN ROY.

Rammohun Roy had long wished to visit England with the view of obtaining as he himself said, "by personal observation a more thorough insight into the manner, customs, religion and political institutions of Europe." He died there in 1833.

After Rammohun Roy went to England, the Society which he

founded began to languish. It was managed by pandits, and become more and more Hinduised. It would have ceased to exist, had it not been supported by the Raja's wealthy friend, Dwarakanath Tagore.

In 1839 Debendranath Tagore founded a "Society for the Knowledge of Truth," which was in 1848 incorporated with that established by Rammohun Roy. After careful investigation, the infallibility of the Vedas was given up in 1850, and the Society became a purely Theistic Church, without any acknowledged Scriptures. Debendranath did not break with caste and Hindu society, although he timidly taught that both needed reformation.

In 1857 Keshub Chunder Sen, then 19 years of age, joined the Society. He had received a good English education, and was a great admirer of the works of Theodore Parker, an American writer. He worked for some years as assistant minister to Debendranath; but in 1865, no longer able to bear the inconsistency of holding the unity of God and the brotherhood of man along with the institution of Hindu caste, he broke away from the old Brahmo

KESHUB CHUNDER SEN.

Samaj, and formed one of his own. He adopted many of the leading terms of Christianity, but gave them a different meaning.

In 1877 Keshub had his daughter married to the young Maharaja of Kuch Behar, contrary to the rules which he had himself laid down. This led to the secession of some of the leading members, who formed a new Society, called the Sadharan (general) Brahmo Samaj. In 1881, Keshub, with some of his remaining followers, started what he called the "New Dispensation," which, in further imitation of Christianity, had its apostles and a kind of baptism. His mind latterly seems to have been affected. He professed to speak in the name of the Lord, and issued a proclamation from "India's Mother."

After Keshub's death in 1884, the Society which he founded was torn by internal dissensions. Mr. P. C. Mozoomdar should have been its leader, but the members refused to allow him to occupy the *vedi* or seat from which Keshub addressed them. The Sadharan Brahmo Samaj, now has most life, although even it is not vigorous. The Adi or original Samaj, to which Debendranath belongs, may be said to have merely a nominal existence.

The members of the Bramho Samaj hold much more enlightened views on the subject of religion than Hindus; but past experience shows that they will probably either return to Hinduism or become Christians. No system of simple theism has ever become a national religion.

THE ASSAMESE.

The **Assamese** inhabit a long narrow valley, watered by the Brahmaputra. Assam formed part of the ancient kingdom of Kamrup, which was overthrown by the Muhammadans in the 15th century. After a time the Kochs, an aboriginal tribe, made themselves masters of the country. In their turn they were subdued by the Ahams, a tribe of the some stock as the Siamese. The Ahams, in danger of being exterminated by the Burmese, asked the English to interfere. Assam was annexed to British India in 1824, after the first Burmese war.

According to the Census of 1891, Assamese was spoken by 1,435,820. The language so much resembles Bengali, that by some it is considered a mere dialect.

The Assamese are a very mixed race. They are distinct from the great body of the Hindus, though in recent times they have adopted the Brahmanical religion. In features they resemble the Siamese. Beverley describes them as "a proud, haughty and indolent people; the use of opium to which they are addicted, having, it is said, an injurious influence upon the national character."* Some efforts have recently been made to lessen the use of opium among them. The Province is being opened up by steam navigation and railways.

CHRISTIAN MISSIONS.

Serampore Mission.—The Serampore missionaries printed the New Testament in Assamese in 1810, and the whole Bible in 1832. Mr. Rae, a Scotchman who had lived several years in Assam, was set apart by Dr. Carey in 1829 to missionary work in that country. He settled at Gauhati, and seems to have been useful; but the mission was not maintained.

American Baptist Mission.—The Rev. Messrs. Brown and Cutter from Burma, the first missionaries of this Society to Assam, arrived at Sadiya, in March, 1836, having been 4 months on the journey from Calcutta. In June a school was opened. The Rev. Messrs. Bronson and Thomas sailed from America in October 1836, taking printing materials with them. Mr. Thomas was killed by a tree falling across his boat when going up the river. Several translations were made and books printed both in Assamese and Khamti. Sadiya was given up in 1839, in consequence of a disturbance which scattered the Khamtis. The first Assamese convert was baptized in 1841, in which year also Sibsagar and Nowgong were occupied: Gauhati was taken up in 1843.

The Baptist missionaries printed improved editions of the Scriptures and published several other works. The *Orunodoi*, a monthly religious paper, was commenced in 1846.

In 1890 there were 9 American missionaries, 1731 communicants, and about 4,500 Native Christians connected with the Mission; but Garos and Nagas are included as well as Assamese.

S. P. G. Mission—A local mission was commenced at Tezpore by the Rev. C. Hessalmeyer about 1850, which was taken up by the Gospel Society in 1862. After his death in 1871, the Rev. S. Endle took charge. Though generally single-handed, the work has prospered under his direction.

In 1893 at Tezpore and Dibrughur, there were 430 communicants, 1,600 baptized persons, and 365 pupils in schools. Some of the Christians are from Chota-Nagpore, employed as coolies on tea plantations.

THE NAGAS.

The Nagas, 100,000 in number, occupy the hills to the north-east of Cachar. Their features are like the Burmese; they have flat noses, and high cheek bones. Their dress consists of a dark blue kilt, ornamented with cowry shells. The most coveted decoration

---

* Bengal Census of 1872, p. 145.

is a neck collar, made of goat's hair dyed red, fringed with the long scalps of slain enemies. The national weapons are a spear, a shield, and a *dao,* or bill-hook. When proceeding on a foray, they carry a large stock of pointed bamboos, a few inches in length, intended to be stuck in the ground, to delay the pursuit of an enemy. They are brave in war, but also treacherous and vindictive. If one of their number is slain, nothing will pacify them till revenge s taken.

The Nagas are very superstitious in the matter of omens. All

NAGAS.

their ceremonies and sacrifices are intended to appease the wrath of numerous evil spirits.

Their funeral ceremonies are very singular. When death occurs from lingering illness, a platform is raised within the house on which the body is placed and watched day and night. When the illness has been short, the platform is erected in a neighbouring jungle, and the corpse folded in cloths, is placed on it and left to decay. When six months have expired, the funeral ceremonies are performed. A large gathering of the friends takes place; music and dancing are continued through an entire day and night, with laments and death songs, brandishing of spears, and imprecations of the evil spirit, who, they suppose, had taken away their friend.

The Naga Hills, forming the south-eastern portion of Assam, were formed into a separate district in 1867. The Nagas continued to make raids upon the neighbouring districts till 1881, when a regiment was stationed at Kohima, and the district was administered as British territory, since which the Nagas have been peaceful.

There are several Naga tribes. The American Baptist missionaries commenced a mission among the Angami Nagas. Kohima was occupied in 1881, and in 1885 a new mission was opened at Wokha, among the Lhota Nagas.

MIKIRS.

The Mikirs, numbering 90,000, inhabit the lower hills, about a day's journey from the plains, south of the Brahmaputra, near the middle of Assam. They are the most peaceful and industrious of the hill tribes. They live in solitary huts, or small hamlets, as many as 30 individuals sometimes occupying the same house. They carry on a brisk traffic with Bengali traders, bartering their cotton, silk, and various jungle products for salt and cloth.

Mission work was commenced among them by the American Baptists. The first convert was baptized in 1863.

KHASIS.

The Khasi tribes, about 180,000 in number, inhabit the hills south of Gauhati and east of the Garos. Their country is remarkable as containing Cherrapunji, with the greatest known rainfall in the world. The hills contain fine limestone, which is exported in large quantities to Calcutta.

The language is monosyllabic, and, so far as yet known, peculiar. The following is a specimen :—

Naba kumta U Blei u la íeit ia ka pyrthei, katba u la aitínoh ia la U Khún ia u ba-la-khámarwei, ba uei-uei-ruh u bangeit ha u, u'n 'nu'm jot shub, hinrei u'n ioh ka jingim b'ymjiukut.

As in some other tribes, the wife is regarded as the head of the family. The husband marries into the wife's family. Property brought by the husband to the wife's house, reverts to his own family at his death. The Khasis bury the ashes of their dead under four upright stones, covered over by a fifth on the top. The same practice was observed in some parts of ancient Europe; but the skeletons were sometimes enclosed—not the ashes.

The Khasi and Jaintia Hills, to the eastward, are under the same Deputy Commissioner. On account of the excessive rainfall at Cherrapunji, the headquarters were transferred from it to Shillong.

Welsh Mission.—Mission work among the Khasis has been carried on by missionaries from Wales. The Rev. Thomas Jones, the first missionary, arrived in India in 1840. Cherrapunji was occupied in 1841. At present the mission field is divided into 9 districts, 8 in the Khasi and Jaintia Hills, and one in Sylhet. At Cherrapunji there are a Normal School and Theological Institution; at Shillong there is a High School. Several of the boys have passed the entrance and obtained scholarships.

Besides tracts, school and religious books, the New Testament and other portions of Scripture have been published in Khasi. The first Khasi periodical, *The Carrier of Tidings*, was issued in 1889.

In 1890 there were connected with the mission 9 Foreign Missionaries, 6190 Native Christians, and 1980 Communicants.

THE GAROS.

The Garos, about 145,000 in number, inhabit the western end of the chain of mountains between the Surma and Brahmaputra valleys.

The Garos are a robust active race, of about the middle height, and of a dark brown colour. Their cheek bones are prominent, noses broad, lips thick, ears large, and eyes of a light brown colour. The men are remarkable for deficiency of beard, whatever hair grows on the face being carefully plucked out. The hair of the head of both sexes is never cut, but either tied up in a knot, or kept off the face by means of a piece of cloth.

Both men and women are inordinately fond of personal ornaments. The males wear 3 or 4 brass ear-rings, and as many bead necklaces as they can afford. Men of hereditary rank wear an iron or brass armlet above the elbow, and a peculiar ornament round the head, which consists of brass plates connected by a string. This lost, it is said can only be assumed by one who has slain an enemy in battle.

The women wear, besides necklaces of glass and bell-metal, beads, and ear-rings of enormous size and weight. It is a coveted mark of distinction to have the lobe of the ear altogether torn away by the strain thus caused, in which case the ear-rings are suspended from a string passed over the top of the head.

In food the Garos eat not only beef and pork, but also tigers, dogs, snakes and frogs. Their staple diet is rice, and their drink rice beer. Milk they altogether eschew, as do all the hill tribes between the Surma and Brahmaputra. They are great smokers of tobacco, but touch no intoxicating drug.

The dead among the Garos are burned, and the ashes buried near the hut door. At the time of cremation, dogs are sacrificed in order that they may direct the spirit on its way. Up to a very recent period, human victims were offered on the occasion of the death of a chief. If no slaves were available, a raid was made into the plains to bring back heads. The skulls were hung up in their houses, and he who had most was held in the highest honour. It was chiefly to stop their head-hunting expeditions into British territory that in 1866 the Garo Hills were annexed. The expenditure is still about double the revenue.

The Garos, like other aboriginal tribes, believe in the existence of witches and imps of all kinds. They have the curious idea that certain persons are capable of leaving their human frames, and taking up their abode in the body of a tiger or other animal. At their funerals, all men, women, and children get drunk.

Mission.—Work among the Garos has been carried on by the American Baptist Missionaries in Assam. The first Garo convert was baptized in 1863. In April 1864 two Garos who had been baptized at Gauhati, were sent to preach to their own people. In 1867 the Garos were first visited by the missionaries, and a church of 40 members was organised at Goalpara. Schools were established and itinerations made. By October 1874, no less than 446 Garos had been baptized. In 1878 a station was found at Tura, the headquarters of the Garo work. A monthly newspaper in Garo was begun in 1880. The four Gospels and some of the epistles have been printed in Garo.

LEPCHAS.

The Lepchas are a small tribe inhabiting Sikkim, a mountainous district in the Himalayas, due north of Calcutta. The number in British territory at the census of 1891 was 10,125. The Lepcha features are somewhat like the Burmese. The face is broad and flat, the chin beardless, the skin yellowish. In disposition the Lepchas are timid and peaceful.

The hair, an object of pride and care, in the dressing of which a female will assist a male, is collected into a large tail—simple or plaited, flat or round. The women wear two tails.

Their religion consists in sacrificing to *evil* spirits. They acknowledge the existence of *good* spirits, but say, "Why should we sacrifice to *them?* They do us no harm. The evil spirits who dwell in every rock, grove, and mountain are constantly at mischief, and to them we must pray, for it is they who hurt us." They may also be called semi-Buddhists.

LEPCHA WATER-CARRIER.

Missions.—Christian labour among the Lepchas was commenced by the Rev. W. Start, a wealthy clergyman of the Church of England, who, at his own expense, brought out in 1841 some German missionaries. With the assistance of the Rev. W. Niebel, he translated the Gospels into the Lepcha language, and printed them at his own cost. The Rev. J. C. Page, of the English Baptist Society, was a zealous labourer among the Lepchas, and erected for them a neat little church at Darjeeling. The work among them is now carried on by missionaries of the Church of Scotland. Darjeeling was first occupied in 1870; Kalimpong, east of the Tísta, was acquired from Bhutan in 1864. It was taken up by the Mission in 1873. The Scottish Universities' Mission to Independent Sikkim was commenced in 1886.

In 1893 there were 6 European missionaries, 2200 converts, of whom one in three is a communicant; and 80 schools, with 2500 pupils. At Kalimpong there is a Training Institution, the students consisting of Lepchas, and Nepalis in about equal numbers.

Of the converts about 1000 are Nepalis, 1000 Lepchas, the remaining 200 are mixed, but chiefly Dhangars. Increasing attention is being devoted to the Nepalis. The Bible is being translated into their language.

THE ORIYAS.

The ORIYAS inhabit the province of ORISSA, which lies along the coast to the south-west of Bengal. The area is 24,000 square miles—about one-third of the size of Bengal—but the population is only about 5 millions. A great part of the interior consists of rugged hills, covered with jungle, and occupied by wild tribes.

The Oriya language is very like Bengali. It is the only one of the North Indian characters which has adopted the curved form of the upper strokes. This was necessary from writing on palm leaves with an iron pen; straight lines would have cut the leaf. It was spoken in 1891 by 9,010,957.

ORIYA, or Uriya. (*Orissa.*)

ଯେହେତୁ ତାହାଙ୍କଠାରେ ପ୍ରତ୍ୟେକ ଜଣ ବିଶ୍ୱାସକାରୀ ଯେମନ୍ତ
ନଷ୍ଟ ନ ହୋଇ ଅନନ୍ତ ପରମାୟୁ ପାଇବ ଏଥିପାଇଁ ଈଶ୍ୱର ଜଗତକୁ
ଏତେ ପ୍ରେମ କଲେ ଯେ ସେ ଆପଣା ଅଦ୍ୱିତୀୟ ପୁତ୍ରକୁ ଦେଲେ ।

For a long time the province was greatly neglected. In some inland parts, a cart is nearly as great a novelty as a balloon. The people are, in general, ignorant, apathetic and superstitious. Many Oriyas are employed in Calcutta as servants. Things are gradually improving. Schools are being established; there is a college at Cuttack. The coast railway will traverse the province, and bring it into easy communication with Calcutta and Madras.

Orissa is chiefly noted for its temple of Jagannath, a form of Krishna, at Puri, a famous place of pilgrimage. The idol has only a head, trunk, stumps for arms. It has well been described as a "hideous caricature of the human face divine." The temple and cars contain sculptures disgustingly obscene. Pilgrims come to the temple from all parts of India.

IMAGE OF JAGANNATH AT PURI.

At Puri they are allowed to eat only the food offered to the idol, which is often badly cooked and unwholesome. The water in the sacred tanks is very filthy. Numbers of the pilgrims die. Skeletons lie scattered along the sides of the roads on the principal routes.

CHRISTIAN MISSIONS.

English Baptist Missions.—About the beginning of the present century, the Rev. Dr. Claudius Buchanan visited Orissa, and his account of the temple of Jagannath excited considerable interest.

The Serampore missionaries opened two stations in Orissa, which they gave up to an English Baptist Missionary Society. Cuttack, the first station occupied by the latter, was commenced in 1822; the following year Puri was added. The human sacrifices of the Khonds in the interior to propitiate the earth-goddess and render their fields fruitful, early attracted the attention of the missionaries. Many children were rescued, and brought up in orphanages. The Orissa missionaries have, as a rule, been familiar with the vernacular, and have travelled much, preaching the Gospel. The mission has been favoured with some remarkable converts. There is an institution at Cuttack for the training of native ministers, and a printing press from which large numbers of Scriptures, school-books, and other publications have been issued. Carey first translated the Bible into Oriya, but a greatly improved version was afterwards made in Orissa. The principal coast stations are now occupied, and one has been commenced at Sumbulpore in the interior.

In 1893 there were connected with the mission 8 English missionaries, 1,137 Church members, 2753 Christian adherents, and 902 pupils under instruction.

American Baptist Mission.—The Rev. Messrs. J. Phillips and Eli Noyes were the first missionaries sent out. Balasore was occupied in 1836; afterwards other stations were taken up. At Midnapore, through Dr. J. L. Phillips, a Bible School for training native helpers was opened in 1879. There is also a Mission Press at the same station. In the northern part of the mission field, Santals are numerous, and considerable success has been met with among them.

In 1891 the Society had 10 American missionaries, 805 Church members and a Christian community of 1363, including both Oriyas and Santals.

THE SANTALS.

The Santals are scattered over a curved strip of country, about 350 miles in length, extending from the Ganges to the river Baitarani. In the western jungles they are the only population; but generally they are mixed with the Hindus of the plain.

The Santal is more squarely built than the Hindu, with a forehead not so high, but rounder and broader. The language belongs to a class called Kolarian, differing both from the northern and southern languages of India. Its grammatical forms are very complete, though it has no written character of its own. It is now printed both in Nagari and Roman. A specimen is given below:

Nonká báṛe ápe hoṉ hoṛko samáṉgre marsál gṉel ochoitápe jemon unko hoṉ ápeá :·bugi kámi gṉelkáte áperen sermáren ja: námi : ko sarhaue.—(*Matt.* v. 16.)

Santali was spoken in 1891 by 1,642,154.

The Santals know no God who will reward the good, but a host of demons ever at hand to scatter disease, to spread murrain among cattle, to blight the crops, unless they are bribed by offerings and bloody sacrifices.

Nearly till the end of last century, the Santals were the pests of the neighbouring plains. Regularly after the December harvest they sallied forth from their mountains, plundered the lowlands, and then retired with their spoil to their jungles. The low country bordering on the hills was almost depopulated, and travellers could not pass with safety.

The earliest efforts to civilise the Santals were made by a young

SANTAL CHRISTIANS.

civilian, named Cleveland. He made liberal presents to the chiefs, and appointed as officers many of their relations. Headmen received salaries to deliver up all criminals to be tried by an assembly of the chiefs. Cleveland died at the early age of 29, but his name was long held in reverence.

In course of time, Hindu money-lenders went among the hills; and the Santals learned to borrow. Before the middle of this century, many of them were plunged in debt. Threatened with imprisonment in a distant jail, in 1855 the Southern Santals started in a vast body, 20,000 strong with their bows and arrows, to walk to Calcutta, 200 miles distant, to lay their grievances before the Governor-General. Robberies took place, and the rising was put down not without some bloodshed. Their wrongs, however, were then fully inquired into, changes were made, and the Santals have, for years, been among the most prosperous of the Indian races.

Christian Missions.

American Baptist Mission.—This Society, labouring in the north of Orissa and the south of Bengal, has a Santal Training School and about 70 Primary Schools in the Santal country. Santal Christians are not given separately in the Report.

Church Mission.—The Church Missionary Society commenced work in Northern Santalistan in 1862. Two Missionaries, the Rev. E. L. Puxley and the Rev. W. T. Storrs, laboured among them with great zeal, and so won their hearts that they were induced by hundreds to place themselves under religious instruction. Mr. Puxley was the first to reduce Santali to writing. He published a valuable dictionary, and also the Gospel of Matthew. Other portions of Scripture, besides a Bible History and school books, have since been published.

The Bishop of Calcutta, when he visited Taljhari the principal station in 1872, ten years after the commencement of the Mission, found a very large and crowded congregation in a church beautifully situated, and very solidly built. The normal and other schools were in excellent order and well taught. In the evening there was a great feast, at which about 800 guests sat down. The singing was sweet.

In 1893 there were 6 English missionaries, 1059 communicants, 3520 baptized or catechumens, and 1170 scholars connected with this Mission.

Indian Home Mission.—This Mission was commenced in 1867 by the Rev. Messrs. Boerresen and Skrefsrud, the one a Dane, the other a Norwegian. It is not connected with any Missionary Society. In 1880 a Santali Christian settlement was formed in Western Assam, which now contains several hundred Christian farmers.

In 1890 there were 6 Foreign Missionaries, and, including about 3500 communicants, a nominal Christian community of 6070 connected with the Mission.

Free Church Mission.—This was commenced in 1871, the work being largely supported by the late Sir W. Mackinnon. There are 3 principal Stations—evangelistic, medico-evangelistic, and educational work being carried on at each.

In 1893 there were three missionaries, two of them medical, 183 church members, 675 baptized adherents, and 1084 scholars connected with the Mission.

Wesleyan Mission.—This Society has a small Santal mission, with 2 evangelists, and 14 church members.

THE TRIBES OF CHOTA NAGPORE.

The table-land of Chota Nagpore is a beautiful region, about 2,000 feet above the level of the sea, about 14,000 square miles in extent, with rivers flowing in every direction. It is inhabited by different tribes, the principal of which will be briefly noticed.

The ORAONS are best known as *Dhangars*, 'hill men', from *Dhang*, 'hill.' In 1891 they numbered 368,222. They are an industrious race, known far and wide as day labourers. Many of them are employed in Calcutta and on tea plantations. Their language belongs to the Dravidian or southern family.

The religion of the Oraons consists in the worship of evil spirits. They think that they please them most by feasting, drinking, and dancing. In every large village there is a dancing ground, surrounded by seats for tired dancers and spectators. During the festive seasons of the year, dancing commences shortly after dark every night, and if the supply of liquor holds out, is often kept up till sunrise.

The name KOLS is often used by Europeans to denote the MUNDARIS and HOS, but it is considered disrespectful, and is not used by the tribes themselves. The Hos in 1891 were included with the Mundaris. Their languages, belonging to the Kolarian family, were spoken in 1891 by 654,507.

The Kols are subdivided into clans, each called after an animal or plant, as snakes, tortoises, and mangoes. A man may not marry a woman of the same clan.

Each Mundari village has a chief called a *múnda!* 'a head,' a name applied to the whole tribe.

Some of the women wear very heavy bracelets, armlets and anklets of bell metal. On the division of property sisters are allotted to the brothers like cattle. The price of a wife is usually 6 head of cattle.

KOL DANCE.

The Kols eat beef, mutton, fowls and fish. In regard to cooked rice they are very particular. They will leave off eating if a man's shadow passes across their food.

Dancing and cock-fighting are their favourite amusements. All disease in man or animals is attributed to the anger of some evil spirit or to the spell of some witch. In the latter case a witch-finder is employed to find out who cast the spell. In former times the person accused and all his family were put to death, in the belief that witches breed witches.

CHRISTIAN MISSIONS.

Gossner's Mission.—Pastor Gossner, the founder of this Mission, was originally a Romish priest, but afterwards became a director of the Berlin Missionary Society. Differing in his views about a missionary's qualifications, he withdrew in 1836, and formed a Society of his own. The first missionaries tried to support themselves by manual labour, but most of them were soon cut off. In 1844 six missionaries were sent to India to labour among the tribes of Chota Nagpore. They visited the people in their villages, they laboured in their own gardens to support themselves, they erected their own buildings; they were heedless of the changes of the climate, and of the intense heat of an Indian sun. One after another, four fell a sacrifice to exposure and over-exertion. The zeal of the remaining two did not flag. In 1850 the first-fruits were gathered. That year they baptized 11 adults, the next 27, and each year the number increased. In 1837 there were upwards of 800 Christians scattered over a great many villages. This result had not been obtained without much opposition. The houses of converts were plundered by armed bands, their rice-stores carried off, the very roofs of their houses taken away, and money and the women's ornaments forcibly seized.

By 1863 there were 3401 baptized Christians. The following account is given of the gathering of the Christians for their Sunday services and harvest festival:

"A large number of the Christians come in from villages to Ranchi every week for the Sabbath services. They are so numerous that a special *serai* has been erected for their use, which, with its broad verandahs and inner court, can accommodate 600 visitors. They bring all their food, and are merely supplied with firewood at the expense of the Mission. A special festival is held on the first Monday of the year to celebrate their harvest feast. Arrived at the church, every one presented an offering. In the front there was a heap of first fruits. Small boxes for money stood on the table, but the rice offered was poured upon the floor. None came empty-handed; every one, men, women, and children, presented money; but the chief gift was the cleaned rice that had been gathered in their fields. Some brought a handful in a cup; a few brought large baskets with half a hundredweight; others a more moderate quantity. Meanwhile the children in the gallery sang a variety of hymns, accompanied by an organ played by the school teacher of their own people. The offerings went on till all were seated in the church for worship."

The Central Education Institution is at Ranchi, conducted by three Europeans. It is divided into the Boys' School, the Normal School, and the Theological Seminary.

In 1890 there were 18 foreign missionaries and 37,412 Native Christians, of whom 11,472 were communicants, connected with the mission.

S. P. G. Mission.—In 1869 some of the German missionaries joined the English Society for the Propagation of the Gospel. The Society built at Ranchi one of the finest mission churches in India. It is a fine sight to see this large building, which holds nearly 1000 people, quite filled, and to listen to the very hearty singing. In 1875 eight Kols were ordained as Christian ministers. In 1889 the Rev. J. C. Whitley was consecrated the first Bishop of Chota Nagpore. In 1891 the first 5 members of the Dublin University Mission came out to work under the S. P. G.

The Gospels and two epistles have been printed in Mandari.

In 1892 there were 11 English missionaries, 13,081 Christians, 6,385 communicants, 456 catechumens, and 1380 scholars connected with the mission.

HINDUSTANIS.

HINDUSTAN, *the country of the Hindus*, is sometimes used to denote the whole of India. More correctly, it is the country between the Vindhya Mountains and the Himalayas, bounded on the west by the Punjab, and on the east by Bengal. The word Hindustanis is here used to denote the nations using the Hindi and Hindustani languages.

The climate of Hindustan Proper is not so moist as that of Bengal. It is warm in the hot season, but the winter is cold and bracing. The rainfall is insufficient, as a rule, for rice; wheat and different kinds of millet are chiefly grown.

HINDUSTANI GENTLEMAN AND LADY.

On account of the climate and more nourishing food, the Hindustanis are taller and stronger than the Bengalis. Instead of the bare heads of the Bengalis, they wear good turbans to protect them from heat or cold.

Hindi is spoken over an area of about 250,000 square miles, and is the vernacular of about 70 millions. It may be divided into Eastern and Western Hindi. On the boundaries, Hindi melts into the surrounding languages. It belongs to the Sanskrit family, and is generally written in the Nagri character.

HINDI.

क्योंकि ईश्वरने जगतको ऐसा प्यार कियाकि उसने
अपना एकलौता पुत्र दिया किजो कोई उसपर
बिश्वास करे सो नाश नहोय परन्तु अनन्त जी
वन पावे।

Hindustani, or Urdu, is a mixed language. For a long time the Muhammadan conquerors of India spoke Persian, and the conquered, Hindi. By the soldiers and people talking to each other, a camp (Urdu) language was formed, containing a mixture of Hindi, Persian, and Arabic. The Persian character is preferred. Hindustani is the language of the Muhammadan rather than of the Hindu population. It is not peculiar to any district.

HINDUSTANI or URDU.

كيونكه خُدا نے دنيا كو ايسا پيار كيا هي كه اُسنے اپنا
اِكلوتا بيٹا دے ديا تا كه جو كوئي اُس پر ايمان لاوے
هلاك نه هووے بلكه حيات ابدي پاوے

In South India Hindustani differs somewhat from that in the north, and is called Dekhani.

The number speaking Urdu may be roughly estimated at 25 millions.

Religion.—Hindustan is the chief seat of Hinduism. Buddhism originated here about five centuries before Christ. Benares was chiefly a Buddhist city for about 800 years. Sankar Acharya, by his disputations with the Buddhists and his writings, did much to promote the worship of Siva in Benares, and Buddhism disappeared from India. Benares is the most noted place of pilgrimage in the country. It is wrongly supposed that if wicked men die here, they are certain to go to heaven. Krishna is supposed to have lived in the neighbourhood of Muttra on the Ganges, about 30 miles above Agra. Rama is largely worshipped. Ram! Ram! is a common salutation. All sin is supposed to be washed away by bathing in the Ganges.

Christian Missions.

Efforts of Chaplains.—The first Protestant missionary efforts among the Hindustani were made at Chunar, on the Ganges, in 1807 by the Rev. Daniel Corrie, a Chaplain. The Europeans at Chunar were all military, but Mr. Corrie sought also to benefit the people of the country. For this purpose he studied Hindustani. There were several converts, among them a Brahman. Schools were also established, and upwards of 70 children received Christian instruction.

Shortly afterwards the Rev. Henry Martyn came to North India as a Chaplain. His life is so interesting that a short account of it will be given.

Martyn was born in 1781. At Cambridge University he was spoken of as "the man who never lost an hour." A fellow student told him that he ought to read hard, "not for the praise of men, but for the glory of God." Though this seemed reasonable, Martyn did not intend that it should affect his conduct. Before long, however, the importance of religion was shown to him in a manner that he did not expect.

At the Christmas examination, 1799, Martyn was first, the account of which gave great pleasure to his father, who was then in excellent health. In January, Martyn heard of his death. He was led to see the vanity of earthly honours, and to think of that invisible world to which his father had gone, and to which he must one day, he knew not how soon, go himself. He began to read the Bible and pray. Soon he accepted the gracious offers of mercy and forgiveness made by the Lord Jesus Christ, and he found "peace in believing."

Martyn's studies were still pursued with diligence; but the object at which he aimed, and the principles by which he was actuated, were changed. At the chief University Examination his mind was calm, which contributed to his success. Although he had not yet completed his 20th year he attained the highest distinction in the University, that of Senior Wrangler. But did it satisfy? He says, "I obtained my highest wishes, but was surprised to find that I had grasped a shadow." The things of earth cannot meet the desires of the soul. As Jesus Christ said, "Whosoever drinketh of *this* water shall thirst again."

Martyn originally intended to be a lawyer, but now he resolved to be a Missionary to the east, and offered himself to the Church Missionary Society. Circumstances, however, led him to go out as a

Chaplain. He reached India in May, 1806. His friends wished to keep him in Calcutta, but he chose rather to go up-country, where he would be more among the people. He was appointed to Dinapore, near Patna. It can now be reached by rail in 10½ hours, but Martyn had to go up the Ganges by boat, the passage taking 6 weeks.

Martyn's appointed duty was to preach to the Europeans at the station. While labouring zealously for the benefit of his countrymen, he set three other objects before himself—the establishment of schools, preaching in Urdu, and translations. He lived simply, that he might spend more money on schools, and abstaining from wine, it was reported among the people that "the Dinapore padre had become Musalman."

Martyn supported at his own expense 5 schools, and when he had acquired a good knowledge of Urdu, he began preaching in that language. The work in which he took most delight was the translation of the New Testament into Urdu and Persian, with the assistance of munshis. He says "the time fled imperceptibly while so delightfully engaged." The Urdu translation, completed in 1808, was highly admired. The Persian version, which followed, was not considered sufficiently idiomatic. As his health had given way, a visit to England was recommended. Instead of going home directly, he determined to proceed to Persia, that he might improve the translation. At Shiraz, the most noted seat of Persian learning, he successfully finished the work, and had frequent discussions with moulvis in defence of Christianity.

In a very weak state of health, he set out for England. The journey was very trying, and he died at Tokat in 1812. The following were the last words he wrote: "I sat in the orchard, and thought with sweet comfort and peace of my God: in solitude my Company, my Friend, my Comforter. Oh! when shall time give place to eternity! when shall appear that new heaven and new earth, wherein dwelleth righteousness?"

Macaulay, when a student at Cambridge, thus wrote of Martyn's death:—

"Here Martyn lies! In manhood's early bloom,
The Christian hero found a pagan tomb!

. . . .

Onward he journeyed to that happy shore,
Where danger, toil, and shame are known no more."

Among those who heard Martyn preach at Cawnpore was a Muhammadan, named Sheik Sahib. He was struck by what he heard, which he considered both reasonable and excellent. When Martyn had finished his translation of the New Testament into Hindustani, the book was given to Sheik Sahib to bind. He not only bound but read the book. Its perusal led him to wish to become a Christian, and he asked Martyn for baptism. He went to Calcutta, but it was thought desirable that he should have further instruction. After five months' delay, the Rev. David Brown in 1811 baptized him in Calcutta, giving him the name of Abdul Masih, "servant of Christ."

In 1813 Mr. Corrie was appointed chaplain at Agra. He took with him Abdul Masih as catechist, and several Christian youths. Abdul was very zealous, and laboured with such success that before the close of the year 41 persons were baptized. He continued to bear such a high character that in 1825 he was ordained by Bishop Heber, the first Native Clergyman of the Church of England in India. He died in 1827. While on his death-bed he joined in singing a hymn which he himself had composed. The following is a literal translation:

"Beloved Saviour! let not me,
In Thy kind heart forgotten be;
Of all that deck the field or bower,
Thou art the sweetest, fairest flower.

"Youth's morn has fled, old age comes on,
But sin distracts my soul alone:
Beloved Saviour! let not me
In Thy kind heart forgotten be."

Mr. Bowley, a young East Indian, had established several schools at Meerut, 40 miles from Delhi. Mr. Corrie went to Meerut at the beginning of 1814, and was so pleased, that on his departure from Agra Mr. Bowley was requested to take charge of the mission there in conjunction with Abdul Masih. In 1815 Mr. Bowley was transferred to Chunar, where he remained for many years. He published a translation of the Old and New Testaments in Hindi, which remained in circulation for a long time. In respect of idiom, it ranks high.

The Rev. Mr. Fisher, a Chaplain at Meerut, took a warm interest in missions. In 1819 he baptised Prabhu Das, the first sepoy who became a Christian. He was a native officer and bore a high character, but such was then the dread of missions that he had to leave his regiment with a pension. He continued to live consistently with his profession. When questioned by English officers, he stated that two of the men had offered him Rs. 20 a month for life, if he would not become a Christian. When asked, "How could you refuse such an offer?" he replied, "I wanted the salvation of my soul, which money will not buy."

Baptist Mission.—In 1811 the Rev. J. Chamberlain, of the Serampore Mission, commenced a mission at Agra. The following year the first baptism took place. Government was then opposed to missions, and shortly afterwards he was sent back to Bengal. In a few weeks, however, he was able to return to North India to educate a child of Colonel Dyce, the daughter of the Begum Sumroo, of Sirdhana. On account of his preaching, he was again ordered to leave North India.

In 1816 the Rev. W. Smith was sent to commence a mission at Benares, and he continued at his post for 40 years. Among his successors were the Rev. John Parsons, an excellent Hindi Scholar, and the Rev. H. Heinig, who spent 42 years in Benares, preaching the Gospel. Monghyr and Patna was also occupied in 1816.

A mission was commenced at Delhi in 1818, but it was for a number of years without a missionary. In 1856 the Rev. J. Mackay was sent out to take charge of it. The principal working member was an eminent Native Christian preacher, Wilayat Ali, a convert from Islam. When the mutiny broke out in 1857, all the missionaries, ladies included, were massacred. Wilayat Ali, on being captured, boldly declared his faith in Christ. "Yes, I am a Christian," he said to the Muhammadan troopers who had seized him, "and I am resolved to live and die a Christian." His last words before his execution were, "O Jesus, receive my soul!" His widow and one of his daughters who escaped were afterwards employed as Christian teachers. At the end of 1858 the work in Dehli was recommenced by the Rev. James Smith, and since then it has been carried on with vigour. In connection with it, there is a flourishing medical mission.

Gya was taken up in 1857, and Simla in 1864.

In 1893 there were 17 missionaries, a Christian community of 1,350* including 997 church members, and 1,468 pupils at school connected with the Mission.

Church Mission.—Abdul Masih and Mr. Bowley, already mentioned, may be regarded as the first agents of the Church Missionary Society in North India. The mission at Benares was commenced in 1817, through the Rev. D. Corrie. Raja Jaynarayan, in gratitude for restoration to health, established and endowed a school. As it did not prosper, in 1818 he handed it over with all its endowments through Mr. Corrie to the Church Missionary Society. A head-master was appointed the same year, but the Rev. Thomas Morris, the first English Missionary, did not arrive till 1821. The school is now called Jay Narayan's College, and has a large number of students.

Among the Church Missionaries who laboured in Benares may be specially mentioned the Rev. Messrs. Smith and Leupolt, who each spent about 40 years in that city. Mr. Smith undertook the evangelistic work, preaching in bazars, markets, and *mélas*. Mr. Leupolt was chiefly employed in superintending orphanages. After the great famine of 1838, a great number were received and brought up.

Among the converts baptized by Mr. Smith was a Brahman

---

* Exclusive of Delhi.

pandit. He was awakened to the truth when endeavouring to refute it. He hesitated for months, having always before him his father's last look, full of reproach, sorrow and agony. He even went back to heathenism for a time; but he had no peace. He was at last baptized under the name of Nehemiah, 4 years after his first convictions. He was afterwards a catechist, and finally ordained a minister. He is the author of one of the most valuable English treatises on Hindu philosophy, A *Rational Refutation of Hindu Philosophy*, translated from the Hindi original, *Shad Darshan Darpan*.

Gorakpur was taken up in 1823. Mr. Wilkinson established a prosperous agricultural settlement on waste land given by Lord William Bentinck. The mission at Agra was commenced by Mr. Corrie. St. John's College at Agra was founded in 1850 by the Rev. Messrs. French and Stuart. At Secundra, in the neighbourhood, there is a large orphanage. Sir Henry Lawrence invited the Society to take up Oudh, and a mission was commenced at Lucknow in 1858. The same year Allahabad was occupied, where the Divinity School of the mission is now stationed. Jabalpur was taken up in 1878.

In 1893 there were 29 European missionaries, and 5,048 Native Christians, including 1,891 communicants, and 6,270 pupils at school connected with the Mission.

London Mission.—The mission of this Society at Benares was commenced in 1820 by the Rev. T. Adam. Among the later missionaries may be mentioned the Rev. James Kennedy, who laboured here for many years; the Rev. M. A. Sherring, author of *The Sacred City of the Hindus, &c.*, and the Rev. J. Hewlett, a scholarly man whose translations are much admired. A high school is maintained, which is well attended. Mirzapur was occupied in 1837. The Rev. Dr. Mather, who did much for Urdu Christian literature, was stationed here for many years. Almora, in the Himalayas, commenced in 1850, is noted for its Leper Asylum. Ranikhet is a few miles from Almora.

In 1893 there were 10 English missionaries, 228 church members, 644 adherents, and 2,846 pupils at school connected with the Mission.

S. P. G. Mission.—The Rev. W. Morton and Rev. T. Christian began work at Bhagalpore in 1823. A station was established at Cawnpore in 1832 by the Rev. J. Carshore. The Rev. W. Haycock and Mr. Cockey who were in charge of the mission when the mutiny broke out, fell at their post in June 1857. The Delhi mission was commenced in 1854. In 1857 the Bishop of Madras reported that it was most hopeful and promising. Less than 5 months afterwards, the missionary, the Rev. A. R. Hubbard and three assistant missionaries, Messrs. Sandys, Cocks, and Koch, were murdered by the rebels, and the mission was broken up. But it was soon renewed, and prospered greatly under the late Rev. R. and Mrs. Winter. The latter was a noble worker among the women. In 1877 the mission was greatly strengthened by the arrival of the Cambridge Mission, one of the pioneers of which was the Rev. E. Bickersteth, now Bishop of Japan. Besides preaching and itinerating, the mission has St. Stephen's College under its charge.

In 1893, including the Cambridge missionaries, there were 13 English missionaries, 1,180 Christians, 445 communicants, and 2,523 scholars connected with the Mission.

American Presbyterian Mission.—The Allahabad mission of this church was commenced in 1836 by the Rev. J. McEwen. The following year a church of 12 members was organised. In 1838 he was obliged to retire from ill health, and the Rev. J. Wilson was transferred to Allahabad. After the Rev. J. H. Morrison came to Allahabad, Mr. Wilson removed to Farrukhabad, where a large number of famine orphans were received. In 1839 the Rev. J. Warren came to Allahabad, with a printing press, which he superintended for 12 years. In 1840 he was joined by the Rev. J. Owen, who commenced a high school, and afterwards devoted considerable attention to literary work.

The Rev. J.L. Scott, appointed to Fatehgarh, close to Farrukhabad, found on his arrival there in 1839 that there were 109 orphans. Measures were adopted for their industrial training. In 1848 the Rev. J. F. Ullmann joined the mission. He rendered excellent service as a hymn writer, and by several works in Hindi and Urdu.

During the mutiny four missionaries, with their wives and two children, were killed at Fatehgarh by order of Nana Sahib. About 30 Native Christians, including Dhokal Prashad, the head teacher of the city school, were killed on the parade ground. In no instance, as far as known, did any of the Christians apostatise.

At Saharanpur the mission has a Theological Seminary, and at Dehra Doon a Boarding School which gives a superior education to the daughters of Native Christians.

The press established by this mission has been very useful. The mission has done much for Bible translation and for increasing the supply of Christian literature.

In 1893 there were connected with the Mission 14 missionaries, 489 church members, a Christian community of 1,843, and 3,529 scholars.

German Mission.—This mission was commenced by missionaries of the Berlin Society. Mozufferpore was occupied in 1840; Chapra in 1842; but they were discontinued for a time. In 1855 the late Rev. W. Ziemann made Ghazipore his headquarters, and laboured there till his death in 1881.

In 1890 there were 4 Foreign missionaries, 600 Christians, and 280 communicants connected with the Mission.

American Methodist Episcopal Mission.—The Rev. Dr. Butler, the pioneer of this mission, arrived in India in 1856. Its headquarters were fixed at Bareilly, in the North-West Provinces. Shortly after Dr. Butler had entered on his work there, the Mutiny broke out, and soon extended as far as Bareilly, which quickly fell into the hands of the rebels, and became a hotbed of sedition. Twelve days before the insurrection at Bareilly, Dr. Butler left for the hills, and so escaped the massacre which took place in that city. When peace was restored, he returned to Bareilly, and recommenced the mission there.

The Mission has missionaries in many of the principal cities of India. It has several Orphanages. Much attention has been devoted to Sunday Schools. There are Mission Presses at Lucknow, Calcutta, and Madras, from which numerous publications have been issued both in English and the vernaculars. A good deal has been done for education. At Lucknow there is the Reid Christian College, also the "Woman's College." There are several High Schools. At Bareilly there is a Theological Seminary, numerously attended. Large numbers, chiefly from the depressed classes, have been baptized. The mission has prospered greatly under Bishop Thoburn, aided by some earnest and able men. Among them may be specially mentioned the late Rev. Dr. B. H. Badley. He was mainly instrumental in the establishment of the Lucknow Christian College, and his *Missionary Directory* is a monument of labour, showing his deep interest in the work.

The compiler has been unable to obtain detailed statistics of the Mission. Dr. Badley's *Indian Missionary Directory* gives the following statistics for 1890: Foreign missionaries 28; Native Christians 19,412; communicants, 9,728; scholars in day schools, 19,341.

Wesleyan Mission.—This Society commenced work at Lucknow in 1872; Benares was occupied in 1879; Faizabad and Jabalpur were afterwards taken up. At all the stations much attention is given to the soldiers and other work in English.

In 1893 there were 4 English missionaries, 156 English and 115 Native church members, and 1,188 day scholars connected with the Mission.

Original Secession Mission.—This Scottish Mission dates from 1872. Seoni, in the Central Provinces, is the only station occupied.

In 1890 there were 3 missionaries, and 56 Native Christians, of whom 8 were communicants.

Canadian Presbyterian Mission.—This mission was commenced at Indore in 1877. Other stations were afterwards occupied. There is a College at Indore, and a Printing Press at Rutlam.

In 1890 there were 7 Foreign missionaries, 172 Native Christians, and 91 communicants.

RAJPUTANA.

Although Hindi, or dialects of it, are spoken throughout this large province, it deserves separate notice on account of the character of its people.

The area of Rajputana is about 130,000 square miles—rather

RAJPUTS.

more than that of the Bombay Presidency. The population is about 12 millions. A small district in the centre is under British rule; the rest is portioned among 20 Native States.

The Rajputs are tall, strong, brave, and proud. They are divided into a number of tribes, formerly so often at war with one another that every man went about armed. From their want of union, they fell successively under the Muhammadans and Mahrattas. The British Government delivered them from the oppression of the latter, and tribal wars have ceased. The country is now being opened up by railways.

Sati and female infanticide formerly prevailed to a large extent. Female infants were often put to death as soon as they were born to avoid the enormous expense foolishly incurred at marriages. Both *sati* and infanticide have been prohibited, and there is a successful movement among the Rajputs themselves to reduce marriage expenses.

MISSIONS.

United Presbyterian Church of Scotland.—The first Christian mission to Rajputana was commenced by this church in 1860. Its pioneer was the Rev. Dr. Shoolbred. Beawar was first taken up; next Ajmere and Nusseerabad. The capitals of the Native States, Jeypore, Jodhpore, Oodeypore, Kotah and Ulwar are now occupied. The prominence given to medical work is one feature of the mission. Dr. Valentine was successful in curing the Maharani of Jeypore, which led to his settlement for some years in that city. Land for a hospital was given at Oodeypore by the Maharana, the Rajput Prince of highest rank. At Ashapoora, near Nuseerabad, there is an orphanage and agricultural settlement. At Ajmere there is a Mission Press. There is also a large female agency.

In 1893 there were 19 missionaries, 1,253 Native Christians, 521 communicants, and 4,553 scholars connected with the Mission.

S. P. G. Mission.—This Mission was commenced in 1886 by the transfer of the Rev. Tara Chand from Kurnaul to Ajmere, as several Native Christians connected with the Church of England had settled in Rajputana.

In 1892 there were 156 Christians, 44 communicants, and 76 scholars.

PANJABIS.

The PANJAB (Five Rivers) now forms the north-western province of India. It contains 106,000 square miles, and is thus nearly equal in size to the North-West Provinces and Oudh. The northern and western frontiers are mountainous; but the province consists chiefly of a large plain, sloping to the south-west. It is watered by the Indus and 5 rivers which fall into the Indus by one channel. The population amounts to 21 millions.

Punjabi is spoken by about 18 millions. By some it is considered to be only an old Hindi dialect; others claim it as a separate language. It employs an old character resembling Nagri, called Gurumukki, because it was at first only employed for taking down the sayings of the Sikh Gurus.

Hindi and Urdu are also spoken by about 6 millions, and Pushtu is the language of Afghans across the Indus.

The bulk of the Punjabi-speaking population resemble those speaking Hindi and Urdu. The chief difference is in the SIKHS, only about one-tenth in number, but important as lately the ruling race. Some account of them will now be given.

The Sikhs.—The Sikhs are a fine stalwart race, numbering nearly 2 millions. Most of them belong to the same stock as the Jats. The word *Sikh,* corrupted from *Sisya,* means disciple. It is used to express the close dependence of the sect on their Gurus.

SIKH.

Nanak, the founder, was born near Lahore in 1469 A. D. His idea was to bring about a union between Hindus and Muhammadans by a belief in one God. But the creed of Nanak was not monotheism (belief in one God), but pantheism (belief that God is all). He taught the repetition of the name of Hari as the only means of salvation.

The tenth Guru converted the Sikhs into a nation of fighting men. His followers were to add *Singh* (lion) to their other names; they were to be distinguished by long hair, to carry a sword, and to wear short trousers.

The sacred book of the Sikhs is called *Adi-Granth*, 'Original Record.' In the Golden Temple at Amritsar it is worshipped.

The Sikhs ascribe great sanctity to the cow. At one time in the Punjab it was a far greater crime to kill a cow than to kill a daughter.

Sikhs may drink wine, but they must refrain from tobacco. Its use would destroy all the merit previously acquired.

The Sikh power reached its greatest height under Ranjit Singh, who gradually extended his conquests till they included the whole of the Punjab and Kashmir. On his death in 1839, the country was torn by dissensions, and the soldiers became unmanageable. In 1845 a large Sikh army invaded British territory. Four bloody battles were fought, after which the Sikhs were driven across the Sutlej. A part of the country was then annexed. In 1848 there was another rising of the Sikhs, and after two great battles, the whole country was made a British province. Delhi was transferred to the Punjab in 1858.

The Sikhs were the most gallant foes the English ever encountered in India, but they are now very loyal to the British Government, and during the Mutiny they rendered essential service.

Arya Samaj.—This recent phase of Hinduism originated with Dayanand Sarasvati, born in the Bombay Presidency; but it is described under the Punjab as it has there received its greatest development.

Dayanand accepted and rejected what he pleased of the Hindu sacred books, and put his own meaning upon them. All the commentaries prepared during the last 20 centuries were wrong: he alone was right. The following were his principal opinions: The eternity of the Vedas; a belief in one God; the eternity of souls and Prakriti; transmigration; the rejection of sacrifice. Caste was denounced, but his followers were not to take food from the hands of Christians or Muhammadans. The Vedas were to be the great object of study for at least 24 years. The allowable ages for marriage were for men from 25 to 48; and for women from 16 to 25.

Numerous Societies have been formed in North India and the Punjab, called Arya Samajes, professing to follow Dayanand's interpretation of the Vedas. An Anglo-Vedic College has been established at Lahore, and a weekly newspaper in English, called the *Arya Patrika,* is issued.

CHRISTIAN MISSIONS.

American Presbyterian Mission.—Work in the Punjab was first commenced by this mission. The pioneer was the Rev. J. C. Lowrie, who settled at Ludhiana, near the east bank of the Sutlej, in 1834. The following year he was joined by the Rev. Messrs. John Newton and James Wilson. In 1837 a Christian church was formed.

In 1846, after the conclusion of the first Sikh war, the mission crossed the first of the five rivers, and settled at Jalandhar. In 1848 Umballa was taken up. The following year, which saw the final collapse of the Sikh kingdom, the missionaries crossed the Beas, and occupied Lahore. From Lahore the Gospel flag was carried across the three remaining rivers, and planted at Rawalpindi in 1856. Other stations were subsequently added.

A good deal of attention has been given to the preparation of Christian literature. A Press was established at Ludhiana in 1836, which sent forth millions of Scriptures and other religious publications. A High School was long conducted at Lahore by the Rev. Dr. Forman, where there is now also a Mission College, largely attended. At Ludhiana there is an Industrial Boarding School. Female education has also received much attention.

Among the missionaries may be specially mentioned the late Rev. Dr. John Newton, distinguished both for his scholarship and Christian character, who laboured for about 50 years in the Punjab. With him may be fitly associated the Rev. Dr. Forman, whose educational work has already been noticed. He came out to India in 1848, and was spared to labour till his death in 1894. Dr. Newton had the privilege of having every one of his sons and daughters, and 4 of his grandchildren in the Indian mission field, and Dr. Forman lived to see 5 of his sons and daughters engaged in the same work.

In 1893 there were connected with the Ludhiana Mission 16 Foreign missionaries, 1180 communicants, and 5426 scholars.

Church Mission.—In the year 1840 a Committee was formed at Simla to establish a Christian mission in the Himalayas. Friends on the spot subscribed liberally. A commencement was made both at Simla and Kotgarh, a station about 25 miles distant. In 1847 these were placed under the Church Missionary Society, its first stations in the Punjab.

In 1849 an Indian officer sent, through the Rev. John Newton, Rs. 10,000 to the Church Missionary Society with a request that missionary work should be commenced in the part of the Punjab which had lately been made British territory. In 1852 the Rev. R. Clark and the Rev. T. H. Fitzpatrick, the first missionaries of the Church of England in the Punjab, settled at Amritsar, the sacred city of the Sikhs. It has a population of about 140,000, and is noted for its famous Sikh Golden Temple. Mr. Clark, one of the founders of the mission was spared to watch over it for upwards of forty years, and largely through his energy, enterprise and devotedness, the work, under God's blessing, has developed remarkably. "The little sapling planted in 1852 has already become a great tree, and has thrown out many branches on every side." In Amritsar evangelistic, educational, medical and zenana work are conducted on a large scale with great efficiency. It has been remarked "that the flower and strength of the country lies in the villages." Very wisely, much attention has been devoted them.

The Church Missions in the Punjab have been deeply indebted to a noble band of lady workers, several of themself-supporting. Among them may be specially mentioned the late Miss C. M. Tucker, who, as A. L. O. E. (a Lady of England), attained a world-wide reputation as an author. In 1875, when 54 years of age, she came out to India as a missionary, and laboured zealously, both with her pen and voice, till her death in 1893.

Miss Tucker died at Batala, a prosperous mission station 24 miles from Amritsar. This was founded and is largely maintained through the liberality of the Rev. F. H. Baring, who laboured for some years as a missionary in India at his own charges.

The late Thomas Valpy French, the first Bishop of Lahore, also

BISHOP FRENCH.

deserves special notice. He first came out to India in 1850, as principal of a College to be commenced at Agra. In 1869 he was appointed Principal of a Divinity School to be established at Lahore, and in 1877 he was consecrated in Westminster Abbey Bishop of Lahore. After holding office for ten years, feeling himself unequal to bear the constant strain, he resigned. He made a short stay in England, during which he studied Arabic to fit himself to labour among Muhammadans. In Lahore he was known as the "seven-tongued man"—one who could speak in seven languages. He went out to Arabia to labour as a missionary. In 1891 he died at Muscat of sun-stroke.

The Rev. Imad-ud-din was a learned Muhammadan moulvie, who sought by repeating prayers 30 times a day, writing out the divine name 125,000 times, etc. to find peace. In 1866 he was baptized at Amritsar. He has since been a great preacher for Christ, and writer of books, chiefly intended to guide Muhammadans to the Saviour.

"Pandit Kharakh Singh, was a learned man who belonged to a great family, and became a Hindu sannyasi. He was sometimes senseless through fastings and exposures, but he was a seeker after God, and he became dissatisfied with his Sanskrit books, because they told him he was God. He heard Nehemiah Goreh preach, and he then bought and read a New Testament that he might prove it false. He thus became convinced of the truth of the Christian religion; and after passing through much agony of mind, he yielded himself to God's service. He was baptized, and afterwards said, 'I now go forth to give my whole life to Christ.' He became a Christian evangelist, going about preaching. He has given a large sum to the mission; though, at the time he gave it, he was living under trees in a hut, or wherever he was led."*

In 1893 there were 33 European missions, 5147 Native Christians, 1006 communicants, and 5323 scholars connected with the Mission. Afghan converts are included, as they are so mixed that it is difficult to separate them.

American United Presbyterian Mission.—This mission was commenced by the Rev. Dr. Andrew Gordon at Sialkot in 1855. The following year two other missionaries arrived, after which educational work and an orphanage were taken up. In 1857 the first two converts were baptized. Other missionaries arrived from time to time, and fresh stations were occupied. There are two Mission High Schools. A Theological Seminary was opened at Sialkot in 1877; a Training Institute in 1881; a Girls' Boarding School in 1878; and a Zenana Hospital in 1888.

In 1890 the statistics of the Mission were as follows: 12 missionaries, 10,162 Native Christians, and 3,788 scholars.

Church of Scotland.—This mission was commenced at Sialkote in 1857. The Chamba Mission, founded by the Rev. W. Ferguson in 1863, was taken over in 1873. Jamu was occupied in 1888.

In 1893 there were connected with the Mission 5 missionaries, 229 communicants, 3,231 baptised Christians, and 2,928 scholars.

TIBETANS.

Tibet, situated to the north of India, forms the highest tableland in the world, the mean elevation being nearly 3 miles above the sea. It is bounded on the south by the Himalayas, and is surrounded on all sides by lofty mountains. It contains several lakes, and the sources of the Indus, Sutlej, and Brahmaputra.

* *Brief Sketches of C. M. S. Missions.*

The cold in winter is very severe. Some grain is raised in the valleys, but the people are mainly pastoral. Sheep, goats, and the *yak*, a kind of buffalo, are the principal domestic quadrupeds.

The Tibetans belong to the Mongolian family. They are strong and hardy. Their religion is a form of Buddhism, mixed up with demon worship and magic. The head of the religion, called the Grand Lama, is supposed to be an incarnation of the coming Buddha.

Great importance is attached to a prayer, called the six-syllabled sentence, *Om mani padme hum*, "Om, the Jewel in the Lotus, Hum." Every Tibetan believes this to be a cure for all evil, a compendium of all knowledge, a summary of all religion. It is supposed that the oftener this formula is repeated, the shorter will be a person's course of transmigration. These six syllables are murmured morning, noon, and night by every man, woman, and child in Tibet.

The words are written or printed on rolls and inscribed in cylinders, to turn round which is thought to have the same efficacy as to have them repeated. If the words are printed a million times, to turn round the cylinder once is equal to repeating them a million times! There are little prayer wheels,

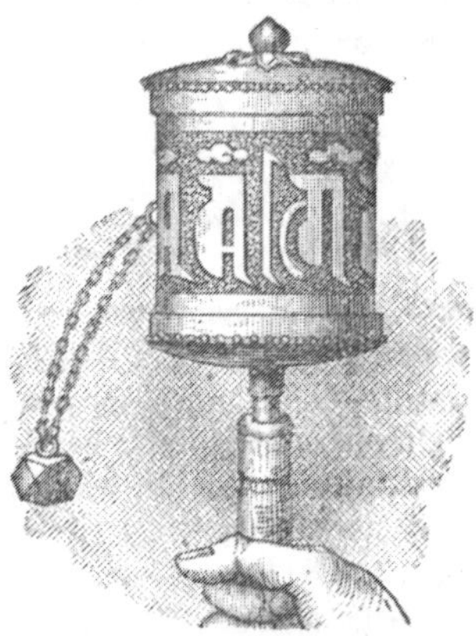

HAND PRAYER-WHEEL.

which the more devout carry with them, turning them round with the hand or a string. All this is useless. God is a Spirit and requires the worship of the heart.

Missions.—Europeans are forbidden to enter Tibet. Some missionaries from Germany have been waiting for years at Kyelang, in the Punjab, on the borders, when there are some Tibetans. For about six months in the year they are shut out by deep snow. During summer there is a post office at the station.

MISSIONARIES AND TIBETANS.

Some years ago there were 23 Christian Tibetans. The New Testament and portions of the Old Testament have been translated.

There are now some English missionaries in India desirous of entering Tibet.

KASHMIRIS.

KASHMIR, or CASHMERE, is a valley in the north-west of the Himalayas, famous for its fine climate and the beauty of its scenery. It forms a basin surrounded on every side by snow-capped mountains, and is a favourite resort during the hot season.

The country has passed through many changes. It was an ancient Hindu kingdom. Muhammadanism was introduced in the 14th century. In 1752 it was conquered by Ahmad Shah, and it remained under Afghan sway till 1819, when it was taken by the Sikhs. In 1846 Ghulab Singh obtained possession of the province as a feudatory of the British Government. About two-thirds of the people are Muhammadans, who tell dreadful tales of the oppression they suffered under the rule of the Sikhs. A recent Maharaja thought that one of his ancestors had transmigrated into a fish. To prevent his being eaten, the use of fish as an article of food was forbidden. Of late the condition of the people has been improved.

The Kashmiris are fair and handsome. Their language belongs to the Sanskrit family, but the Muhammadans use many Persian

KASHMIRI MANNER OF DRESSING THE HAIR.

and Arabic words. Some Brahmans from Kashmir have settled in India, where they are known as "Kashmiri pandits."

Church Mission.—In 1854 the Rev. Robert Clark and Colonel Martin visited Cashmere. They were kindly received by the Maharaja Ghulab Singh, who gave his willing consent to mission work in his kingdom. The Kashmiris, he said, "were so bad that he was quite sure the padres could do them no harm!" Nothing, however, was done till Mr. Clark again visited Cashmere in 1862. The following year the Rev. W. Smith of Benares was sent to

Cashmere, and the mission was permanently established. In 1865 Dr. Elmslie, a medical missionary, was appointed to Cashmere who, through his kindness and skill, soon won a reputation throughout the country. The people flocked in crowds to the Mission Hospital. For a time the work suffered from the opposition of the authorities, but the people themselves were friendly.

The New Testament was translated into Kashmiri by the Rev. R. T. Wade.

In 1893 there were 3 European missionaries, 42 Native Christians, 12 communicants, and 280 scholars connected with the Mission.

Afghans or Pathans.

The **Afghans** consist of various tribes belonging to Afghanistan, but of whom nearly a million are found in the north-western frontier of the Punjab.

As a race the Afghans are athletic, often with a flowing beard, prominent cheek bones, a high and hooked nose. The hair is shaved off from the forehead to the top of the head, the remainder at the sides being allowed to fall in large curls over the

AFGHANS.

shoulders. Their step is full of resolution, their bearing proud, and apt to be rough. The women are rigidly secluded.

The hill tribes are Muhammadans of the worst type. Many of them are so ignorant that they cannot tell even the name of their prophet. Blood for blood, and fire and sword against infidels, are their ruling ideas. Each tribe has its internecine wars, each family its hereditary blood feuds, and each individual has personal foes. They are passionate in revenge, which they will satisfy in the most cruel manner even at the cost of their own lives. To guard against this, they are generally armed, even when grazing cattle, driving beasts of burden, or tilling the soil. When the Peshawar valley came under British rule, there was a murder, on an average, every day. In British territory Afghans are becoming more orderly, and even in Afghanistan there is some improvement.

The language, called Pushtu or Puktu, is Aryan, but it has borrowed many words from Persian and Arabic. Afghans often visit India as traders. Many of them are notorious for their want of cleanliness.

Missions.—These owe their commencement to Major Martin. His regiment was ordered to Peshawar, and he had not been long there when he asked the Commissioner to sanction the establishment of a mission. The latter refused on account of the fanaticism of the people. This Commissioner was in a few months afterwards assassinated. In 1853 the Rev. Robert Clark was invited to Peshawar. The Commissioner was Sir Herbert Edwardes. He took a different view from his predecessor, He said: "I have no fear that the establishment of a Christian Mission at Peshawar will tend to disturb the peace." In a few weeks the sum of Rs. 20,000 was raised for the support of a mission.

The first missionaries to Peshawar were the Rev. Dr. Pfander from Agra, the Rev. R. Clark from Amritsar, and Major Martin who left the army to become a missionary.

Dr. Pfander began to teach and to preach. He was told that if he did so, he would be killed, but he went on preaching. Although several officers have been murdered by Afghans, no missionary has ever lost his life through them.

Soon after the establishment of the Church Mission, the Rev. J. Lœventhal, a converted Jew of the Presbyterian mission, came to Peshawar. He had an excellent knowledge of Pushtu, and translated the New Testament into that language. In 1864 he was accidentally shot.

Peshawar was formerly unhealthy, and several of the early missionaries died. The work, however, has been maintained. A native church has been gathered, and there is a prosperous English school, besides several vernacular schools.

One feature of the mission is its "guest house." The Afghans consider hospitality one of the chief virtues. Here strangers are entertained.

There are other mission stations on the frontier, through which Afghans are reached. Colonel Reynell Taylor gave £1000 for the establishment of a mission at Bannu, through which many Afghan traders pass. The statistics of the Afghan stations are included in those of the Punjab.

SINDIS.

SIND is a province on the lower course of the Indus, about twice the size of Oudh. Much of it is a desert, cultivation being generally confined to the banks of the river. In some parts the ranges of sand hills succeed one another like vast waves. The population, which is very mixed, is about 2½ millions.

The Sindi language is spoken by about 4 millions in Sind and the Punjab. It is the most intricate of the Aryan languages;

SINDIS.

the genitive particle has 20 forms. Muhammadans write it in the Arabic character, with a few additional letters; Hindus use Gurmukhi or a kind of Nagri.

The Sindis are taller and stronger than the Mahrattas. A peculiar hat, compared to a European hat inverted, is worn by all except religious characters, who prefer the turban. Among the higher classes it has a square top.

The Sindis are one of the most gambling of oriental nations: all sexes and orders appear to have an equal passion for ply. The women are ignorant, and devotedly fond of flattery. Their peculiar ornament consists of large ivory rings, covering the forearm.

Sind was the first province of India which suffered from Arab invasions, and about three-fourths of the Sindis are Muhammadans. They are mostly cultivators. The inhabitants of towns are largely Hindus.

In 1859 the Province contained only 20 Government schools; in 1884 they had increased to 340, with 23,273 pupils.

Missions.—The CHURCH MISSIONARY SOCIETY first occupied Hyderabad, the former capital, in 1848, Karachi was taken up in 1848; Sukkar and Shikarpore were afterwards added. At Karachi the Rev. James Sheldon laboured patiently for 28 years. The Rev. G. Shirt translated part of the Scriptures into Sindi.

In 1893 there were 4 missionaries, 173 Christians, 73 communicants, and 1,046 scholars connected with the Mission.

GUJARATIS.

GUJARATI is spoken by about 10½ millions, chiefly inhabiting the districts around the Gulf of Cambay. The country is watered by the Tapti, Narbada, and other rivers. Gujarat is so fertile that it has been called the "Garden of India."

The greater part of Gujarat is under Native princes, of whom the Gaekwar of Baroda is the most important. Kathiawar is a large peninsula to the westward. Some of the Kathiawar princes are among the most enlightened in India. They have done much for railways and education. The same remark applies to the Gaekwar.

The language is like Hindi, but has a little more Persian. The alphabet is derived from the Nagri, omitting the top line.

GUJERATI. (*Western India.*)

કેમકે દેવે જગત પર એવડી પ્રીતિ કિધી, કે
તેણે પોતાનો એકાકીજનિત પુત્ર એ સારૂ આપ્યો
કે, જે કોઈ તે પર વિશ્વાસ કરે તેનો નાશ ન
થાએ, પણ અનંત જીવન પામે.

Brahmans are found as priests, landowners, headmen, and even as cultivators. There are several tribes of Rajputs, who practised female infanticide till it was suppressed by the British Government. The farmers, called Kunbis, are in general industrious and well clad. One class of them has the curious custom of celebrating their marriages only on one particular day of the year.

The Banyas are mostly Jains in religion. Their oppression of the poor cultivators, to whom they are ever ready to lend money, is well known. There are, however, honourable exceptions.

The Dhers are an extensive tribe scattered over Gujarat, who act as village scavengers, and occasionally as village watchmen. Spinning and weaving are their principal occupations.

A number of Gujaratis, to their disgrace, belong to the infamous Vallabha sect of Vaishnavas. Their high priests, called Maharajas, are regarded as incarnations of Krishna. Men and women prostrate themselves at their feet, offering them incense, fruits and flowers, and waving lights before them. Rich Bombay merchants, as shown at a trial in 1862, gave their wives and daughters to be prostituted as an act of religious merit to men who had ruined their health by dabauchery.

Missions.

Baptist Mission.—The first missionary to enter Gujarat was the Rev. C. C. Aratoon, an Armenian, a convert of the Baptist Mission in Bengal. He came to Surat in 1812, and laboured there till 1821, when he returned to Bengal.

London Mission.—As early as 1804 the London Missionary Society sent out two missionaries, intended to open a mission at Surat, the first British settlement in India; but one was detained at Madras, and the other went elsewhere. In 1815, however, the same Society sent out the Rev. Messrs. Fyvie and Skinner to Surat. They early devoted themselves to the translation of the Scriptures, and established a Mission Press, still known as the "Surat Mission Press." They were the first to translate and publish the whole Bible in Gujarati. They were joined from time to time by other labourers, and fresh stations were occupied. Among the Missionaries may be mentioned the Rev. W. Clarkson, an earnest worker, and the Rev. J. V. Taylor, author of an excellent Gujarati Grammar.

Irish Presbyterian Mission.—In 1841 the Irish Presbyterian Church sent out the Rev. James Glasgow and the Rev. A. Kerr to commence a mission at Rajkot, in the Kathiawar peninsula. Mr. Kerr died within six months, but early in the following year the Rev. James Glasgow was joined by his brother Adam and the Rev. R. Montgomery. The two brothers remained at Rajkot; Mr. Montgomery proceeded to Porbandar. In 1843 a learned Muhammadan embracing Christianity at Porbandar, the Native Government obliged the missionary to leave.

As the London Mission had no other missions except at a great distance, it was felt that the Irish Church could carry on the work more efficiently, and in 1846 the Surat Mission was transferred to it, and its other stations in 1859. Ahmedabad was taken up in 1861. The mission converts being as a rule agriculturists, a settlement was formed at Shahavadi, about 4 miles from Ahmedabad. Other agricultural settlements were subsequently established. In recent years there has been a considerable advance in the number of converts, the formation of congregations, and the erection of churches. There are High Schools at Surat and Ahmedabad, and a Theological Institution.

In 1890 the statistics of the Mission were as follows: Foreign missionaries 11; Native Christians 2,146; communicants 390; scholars 3,375.

MAHRATTAS.

The MAHRATTA COUNTRY, may be described as an irregular triangle. The shore of the Arabian Sea between Damaun and Goa forms the base; the apex is a point in a north-easterly direction some distance beyond Nagpur. The area may be roughly estimated at 110,000 square miles. In 1891 the Mahrattas numbered nearly 19 millions.

Marathi is a copious and beautiful language, second only to Hindi. It has admitted a number of words from Arabic and

MARATHI.

कां तर देवानें जगावर एवढी प्रीति केलीकीं, त्यानें
आपला एकुलता पुत्र दिल्हा, यासाठीं कीं जो
कोणी त्यावर विश्वास ठेवितो त्याचा नाश होऊं
नये, तर त्याला सर्वकाळचें जीवन व्हावें.

Persian as well as from Sanskrit. Konkani is a dialect spoken in the Konkan, the strip of country between the sea and the Western Ghats. The Nagri character, slightly altered, is usually employed in books.

The Mahrattas are a small, but hardy and active race of men. While the Bengalis often go bareheaded, the Mahrattas are noted for their large turbans. They were never so much under Muhammadan influence as Hindus in the north, so the women have far greater liberty. Mahratta ladies move about freely unveiled.

The Mahratta Brahmans are noted for their administrative talent and acuteness. At first they contented themselves with the highest offices under Mahratta rulers; but later, as is well known, the Peshwa and other Brahmans usurped the supreme power itself, assumed the command of armies, and openly ruled the confederacy.

MAHRATTAS.

The agricultural Kunbis are the chief tribe. To them belongs peculiarly the name Mahratta.

The Mahrattas are Hindus; but local deities are the chief objects of worship. Pandharpur, south-east of Poona, is one of the most celebrated shrines. The part of the town where it stands is considered holy, and is called Pandharikshetra, or the holy field of Pandhari. The god is called Vithoba or Viththal. Originally a Brahman, he is now regarded as a form of Krishna. In idols he is represented as standing on a brick, with his arms akimbo, the hands resting on the lips.

Vithoba owes much of his popularity to the songs of Tukaram, the Mahratta national poet.

At Jejuri, 30 miles from Poona, Khandoba, a raja, is looked upon as an incarnation of Siva. He is sometimes represented with his wife on horseback, attended by a dog. A wicked custom prevails of dedicating young girls to the god's service. After undergoing a ceremonial "purification," they are branded with a heated stamp. Although nominally wives of the god, they are simply prostitutes.

At Alandi, a Brahman, called Dnyanoba, is worshipped. He is said to have caused a buffalo to speak and recite a hymn from the Veda!

MISSIONS.

American Board.—The first Protestant Mission in Western India was commenced by this Society. The Rev. Messrs. Hall and Nott, who belonged to the first company of foreign missionaries ever ordained in America, landed at Bombay in 1813. England was then at war with the United States, and the two missionaries were ordered to leave the country. This order was afterwards suspended, and they were allowed to remain. In 1816 a Mission Press was established, the plant consisting of a single wooden press, and a small supply of type obtained from Calcutta. Early in 1817 the first Christian tract ever printed in Marathi was issued. The press became eventually a large establishment and did excellent service to missions, both in providing improved Marathi type and in printing. It was afterwards sold; but the Mission still maintains its useful paper, the *Dnyanodaya.*

Work has been carried on continuously in Bombay, and it has some interesting schools. Ahmednagar, about 120 miles north-east of Bombay, was occupied in 1831 by the Rev. Messrs. Read and Boggs, and it is now the chief centre. There are village stations dotted around, but some other towns above the ghats, as Satara and Sholapur, are also occupied. At Ahmednagar there is an English High School, a Girls' Boarding School, and Theological Seminary. The male teachers of the mission have been trained for about 30 years in the Normal School of the Christian Literature Society under Mr. J. S. Haig. At Sirur there is an Industrial School. Able and earnest men have laboured in connection with this mission. The names of some are happily preserved through their children. In 1893 it was reported that the *twenty-third* had joined the mission.

In 1893 the statistics of this Mission were as follows: Foreign Missionaries 14; baptized persons 4,359; communicants 2,562; scholars 3,759.

Church Mission.—Mr. Kenney, the first missionary of this Society, arrived in 1820. Among other missionaries who followed may be mentioned the Rev. A. Farrar, father of Canon Farrar. The chief features of the work in Bombay are the Money School and the mission among Muhammadans. A mission at Nasik was opened in 1830. Mr. Price opened an Industrial School in the neighbourhood, called *Sharanpur* (The City of Refuge). Liberated African slaves were sent there by Government, and six of them volunteered to go with Livingstone in his last journey. When warned of the dangers, they said, "When our master dies, we will die." Two of them brought home his dead body.

Poona was long the residence of the Rev. Sorabji Kharsedji, a converted Parsi; Mrs. Sorabji's High School for Girls has been very useful. Miss Cornelia Sorabji was the first Indian lady graduate in Western India. The Society has now a Divinity School at Poona.

The Aurungabad Mission has prospered under the superintendence of the Rev. Ratonji Naoroji. In 1856 he was greatly impressed by the preaching of the Rev. Nehemiah Goreh, and gave up good worldly prospects to enter the mission. Not long ago there were 28 catechists preaching in the numerous villages.

Malegaon in Khandesh was occupied in 1848.

In 1894 the Mission had 13 European missionaries; 2,464 Native Christians, 1,098 communicants, and 1,375 scholars.

Scottish Missions.—In 1822 the Scottish Missionary Society opened a station at the Bankot, 60 miles south of Bombay. The Rev. Donald Mitchell, the first missionary, died in 8 months, but before the close of the year three missionaries came out, and in 1823, Harnai, near Severndroog, was occupied. Among them was the Rev. James Mitchell, who was privileged to labour for 43 years. In 1827 the Rev. Robert Nesbit joined the mission, and had a long course of usefulness; but the most distinguished member of the mission was the Rev. John Wilson, who arrived in 1829. After spending some months at the southern stations, Mr. Wilson settled in Bombay. Mr. Wilson was an excellent linguist, and soon acquired a knowledge of Mahratti. The following year he commenced a valuable monthly Periodical in English, called *The Oriental Christian Spectator*. He also wrote two trenchant exposures of Hinduism. In 1835 the Rev. Messrs. Mitchell, Nesbit, and Wilson were transferred from the Scottish Missionary Society to the Church of Scotland.

In 1835 an English School, established by some good men, was transferred to the mission. On the arrival in 1838 of the Rev. J. Murray Mitchell, a distinguished Aberdeen graduate, the school was extended, and became known as the General Assembly's Institution. Shortly after the transfer of the school, a Parsi boy, about 14 years of age, named Dhanjibhai Nauroji, was enrolled as a scholar. The following year another Parsi youth, named Hormasji Pestonji, became a pupil. In 1839 both were baptized, after repeated attempts of the Parsis to carry them off by violence. Of 284 pupils in attendance, all but 50 were taken away, and those who remained were chiefly Christians. But the institution soon regained its former strength, although the Parsis kept aloof. In 1843 Mr. Wilson published a large and complete exposure of Zoroastrianism.

In 1843, Dr. Wilson went home on furlough, taking with him Dhanjibhai that he might complete at Edinburgh his studies for

REV. DR. JOHN WILSON.

the ministry. On his way home Dr. Wilson visited Palestine, an account of which he published, entitled *Lands of the Bible*. During the same year the Bombay missionaries seceded from the Church of Scotland, and joined the Free Church of Scotland. The baptism of a Mahratta Brahman, Narayan Sheshadri, one of the best pupils in the institution, also took place. Next day the Brahmans met and resolved to excommunicate all parents who should in future send their sons as pupils. Shripat, a younger brother of Sheshadri, wished to become a Christian and took food at the Mission House, but he was sent back to his father. His relations tried to get him restored to his caste; but the orthodox party decided that this was impossible. This gave great satisfaction to bigoted Hindus. "No such joy," said a Native paper, "was experienced by Brahmans, even when Vishnu, having become incarnate as a fish, rescued the Vedas from the hands of Shurkasur." Narayan Sheshadri died at sea in 1891, after having been instrumental in leading hundreds to embrace Christianity.

In 1847 Dr. Wilson and Dhanjibhai returned to Bombay. Three years later Mr. Murray Mitchell published the first edition of his *Letters to Indian Youth on the Evidences of the Christian Religion*, which has passed through numerous editions* and been very useful.

In 1854, Mr. Baba Padmanji, aged 24, the foremost pupil in the Institution, received baptism at Belgaum. He had commenced his education there, after which he had removed to Bombay to the Free Church Institution to carry it on. On receiving baptism, he returned to Bombay, and became of great value to the cause of Christian Missions in Western India. For 16 years Mr. Padmanji was a teacher, and for 6 years pastor of the native congregation at Poona. Since that time he has devoted himself to literary work. Upwards of 70 publications have proceeded from his pen, among them a Life of Christ, a Commentary on Genesis, and an Annotated New Testament in Marathi.†

During 1855 there were 18 adults admitted into the Native Church, and the following year Ganpat Rao Raghunath, aged 18, a Parbhu, who had been the first pupil at the late examination, was baptized. He was afterwards ordained and laboured for several years at Alibag, south of Bombay.

Dr. Wilson died in 1875, after a long and honourable career as a missionary. His name is preserved in Bombay by the Wilson College, a large and commodious building, with a strong staff of professors.

The Free Church has several other stations in the Bombay Presidency. Poona has been occupied since 1831; at Nagpur is the Hislop College, besides work in the neighbourhood.

In 1893 the Mission had 14 European ordained missionaries, 858 communicants, 512 baptised adherents, and 4,620 scholars.

The Church of Scotland Mission in Western India is now chiefly limited to efforts among the women. Poona is the chief centre.

S. P. G Mission.—During Bishop Heber's visit to Bombay in 1825, a committee of this Society was formed, but little was done till 1840, when the mission of the Rev. G. Candy to the Indo-Britons was taken up. In 1860 the Society sent out a Secretary to organise mission work. Since then the work has gradually extended. The principal fields are Bombay, Ahmednagar, Kolhapur, Dapoli, and Dharwar.

---

* Copies of the 11th edition, greatly enlarged, may be obtained from Mr. A. T. Scott, Tract, Depôt, Madras, Price 6 As. Post-free.

† See his interesting autobiography, *Baba Padmanji*, edited by the Rev. Dr. Murray Mitchell. Sold by Mr. A. T. Scott, Price 2½ As. Post-free, 3 As.

In 1893 the Mission had 11 priests, 5,125 Native Christians, 1,052 communicants, and 1,535 scholars.

American Presbyterian Mission.—This mission occupies the Kolhapur Native State and a part of the coast, called the Southern Konkan. The mission was commenced at Kolhapur in 1852 by the Rev. R. G. Wilder, then connected with the American Board. In 1870 the mission was taken over by the American Presbyterians. The Rev. G. W. Seiler was sent out the same year, and other missionaries followed. Ratnagiri, on the coast, was taken up in 1875.

The Statistical Tables for 1890 give the Natives Christians as 229; communicants 151; scholars 827. Returns were not furnished.

Friends' Mission.—A lady was sent to Benares in 1866, but the work was soon transferred to the Mahratta country. Mr. Charles Gayford came out in 1873, and the following year the mission was moved to Sohagpur. The headquarters were finally fixed at Hoshangabad in 1876. Mr. Samuel Baker joined the mission in 1878, and other missionaries followed; fresh ground being taken up.

In 1890 the mission had 12 European missionaries, 48 members, and 170 scholars.

Faith Mission.—The Rev. M. B. Fuller commenced the Akola Faith Mission in 1884; in 1887 ten ladies were sent from America to commence the Cullis, or South Berar Faith Mission.

Pandita Ramabai.—This remarkableMahratta lady was taught Sanskrit when a child by her mother, while she wandered about with her father who was a pandit. After the death of her parents, Ramabai and her brother continued to travel. She advocated female education, and created a sensation by her scholarship. She was summoned before the assembled pandits of Calcutta, and as the result of their examination, the distinguished title of Sarasvati was publicly conferred on her. Afterwards she married a Calcutta graduate, but he died in 19 months. Ramabai then returned to her former occupation of lecturer. She felt a strong desire to visit England, where she embraced Christianity. Receiving an invitation to visit America, she spent some time in the United States before her return to India. Herself a widow, her efforts have been mainly directed to benefit them. She has established a very interesting Widows' Home at Poona.

BHILS.

The Bhils were formerly a powerful tribe occupying the hills and forests of Southern Rajputana, from which many of them were driven out and settled in the north of the Bombay Presidency. They are distinguished by their dark colour, diminutive size, prominent cheek bones, large nostrils, activity and skill as hunters

In 1891 the Bhil language was spoken by about 150,000. It is ranked as Kolarian, with Santali and Mundari.

Unlike the orthodox Hindu, the Bhils have always eaten the flesh of the cow. In fact, they eat every wild animal except the monkey, which is universally worshipped in the form of Hanuman. It is very curious and shows the antiquity of this race that at the coronation of the highest Rajput Chiefs, in States where Bhils live, the sacred mark of kingship is impressed on the forehead of the new chief by the head of the Bhil family. They take every opportunity of having a feast and a drinking bout. Witchcraft and omens are implicitly believed in; charms of various kinds are universally used.

Sir James Outram made successful efforts to civilise some of the Bhils. He formed a Bhil regiment, which did much to wean them from predatory habits. In 1880 the Rev. C. S. Thompson was appointed by the Church Missionary Society to labour among the Bhils at Kherwara, in Rajputana. Day schools have been opened at six outstations, in which about 200 Bhil boys are instructed up to Standard VI. Several of the Native Princes have shown an interest in them. In 1892 there were 17 baptised Bhils, and 281 scholars.

GONDS.

In old maps of India a large territory was marked GONDWANA, which is now included in the Central Provinces. The Gonds are found in different parts between the Vindhya Mountains and the Godavari. They are about the middle size. They have the dark skin, flat nose, and thick lips which proclaim them of other than Aryan blood. Their dirtiness and the tattoo marks on their faces, arms, and thighs, repel Europeans. They are more truthful than the Hindus, but arrant thieves. All are fond of music and dancing. Like many other aboriginal tribes, they have a strong belief in witchcraft. A man's wife or his child gets sick. Instead of ascribing it to bad food or some such cause, it is put down to witchcraft, and the supposed witch is beaten to death. In some parts there are temples of Kali, where formerly human sacrifices were offered.

In 1891 the Gonds numbered 1,379,580. Their language is reckoned Dravidian. It is remarkable for its numerous grammatical inflections.

The Gonds say they had several lines of kings. There are inscriptions claiming that some of their princes, by their beneficence, made earth better than heaven, and how the sea was swollen by the tears of queens widowed by their conquests!

Missions.—Work among the Gonds seems to have been commenced by the late Rev. James Dawson, of the Free Church Mission. He prepared a Gondi Primer and translated two of the Gospels. The Church Missionary Society sent out the Rev. H. D. Williamson in 1878 to begin a mission among the Gonds at Mandla, in the Central Provinces, He prepared a Gondi Grammar and some other works.

In 1893 there were 6 missionaries and evangelists, 115 Native Christians, 25 communicants, and 61 scholars. Genesis and three gospels have been published in Gondi.

THE KOIS.

The Kois, on the banks of the Upper Godavari, belong to the same race as the Gonds. The following is a specimen of their language:—

KOIS.

Nanna tédi, ná ṭappénagga anji, ó yaipá, nan na Dévuni munne ní munne pápam ṭungi minnána.—(*Luke* xv. 18.)

The general idea of the Kois is that the spirits of the dead wander about the forest in the form of *pishachas*. They do not believe that any one dies what is commonly called a natural death; but always assert that the death of every one is caused by the machinations of a sorcerer, instigated thereto by an enemy of the deceased or of the deceased friends. So, in former years, inquiry was always made as to the person likely to have been at such enmity to the deceased as to wish for his death; and having settled upon a suspicious individual, the friends of the deceased used to carry the corpse to the accused, and call upon him to clear himself by undergoing the ordeal of dipping his hands in boiling oil or water. Reputed wizards and witches are held in great abhorrence, and at times the British rule is complained of as unjust in not allowing these people to be put to death.

The goddess Mamile or Lele must be propitiated early in the year, or else the crops will undoubtedly fail; and she is said to be very partial to human victims.

Wild dogs are regarded as the messengers of the Pandava brothers. On no account would they attempt to kill one of them, even though it should happen to attack their favourite calf.

Mission.—Captain Haig, an Engineer employed on the Godavari works at Dummagudem, and Razu, a Christian convert in the Commissariat, first began mission work among the Kois. They built mission rooms, and Razu resigned his post under Government to labour as a catechist. The first misssionary sent by the Church Missionary Society was the Rev. W. J. Edmonds in 1861. Mr. Darling baptized the first converts in 1869. In 1893 there were 661 Native Christians, 144 communicants, and 148 scholars. But only a few of the Native Christians are Kois.

TELUGUS.

Of all the Dravidian languages, Telugu is spoken over the largest area, and by the greatest number of people. It is current along the eastern coast from near to Madras to Chicacole, where it begins to yield to Oriya. Inland, it extends to about the middle of the peninsula. The area may be roughly estimated at 100,000 square miles. In 1891 the number speaking Telugu was nearly 20 millions. The character is largely circular.

దేవుడు లోకమును ప్రేమించుట ఏలాగంటే, ఆయనయందు విశ్వాసముంచే ప్రతివాడును నశించక నిత్యజీవము పొందే నిమిత్తము తన జనితైక కుమారుని ఇచ్చెను.

The Telugu, in respect of antiquity of culture and glossarial copiousness, ranks next to the Tamil in the list of Dravidian idioms; but in point of euphonic sweetness it claims to occupy the first place. It has been styled the "Italian of the East." Telugu, called also Telinga, is the Andhra of Sanskrit writers, a name mentioned by the Greek geographers as the name of a nation dwelling on or near the Ganges.

Of the five cultivated Dravidian dialects, the farthest removed from each other are the Tamil and the Telugu.

The Telugu people were more enterprising in ancient times than

A TELUGU.

at present. The Klings, who in the early centuries of the Christian era formed settlements, built temples, and exercised dominion in Sumatra and Java, appear to have been Telugus. The ancestors of the Peguans obtained their written character from the Telugus, and from the Peguans the Burmese derived their alphabet.

One of the names by which the Telugu language is known in the Tamil country is *Vadugu,* from *vada,* north, the Telugu country lying to the north of the Tamil.

Malas, called Dhers in Gujarat, and Pariahs in the Tamil country, are numerous.

MISSIONS.

London Mission.—The first missionaries to the Telugu people were the Rev. Messrs. Cran and Des Granges, sent out by the London Missionary Society. They commenced work at Vizagapatam in 1805, at a time when the East India Company was strongly opposed to Missions. They established schools, conversed with the people, and translated some portions of Scripture. Mr. Cran died in 1809, and Mr. Des Granges the following year; but before he was taken away a small native Church had been formed. Two missionaries, Messrs. Gordon and Lee, arrived only in time to receive charge of the mission from Mr. Des Granges.

The mission has been maintained to the present time by a succession of labourers. Messrs. Gordon and Pritchett prepared a version of the New Testament which was printed in 1818. The Old Testament was first printed in 1850.

Among the missionaries who laboured at Vizagapatam may be specially mentioned the late Rev. Dr. John Hay. He did much for education, but his great work was the revision of the Telugu Bible, to which he was set apart during the concluding years of his life. He died in 1891.

About 1840 a Mission Press was established at Vizagapatam, under the Rev. R. D. Johnston, an excellent Telugu scholar, from which Scriptures and other Christian publications were issued.

The Cuddapah Mission was commenced in 1824 by the Rev. W. Howell. Schools were opened and a few converts were baptized, who, in 1833, had increased to 114. For the next 18 years, the work remained nearly stationary. In 1851 several villages of Malas, or field labourers, wished to embrace Christianity. After instruction, many families were baptized. In 1853 the movement extended to the neighbouring district of Kurnool, and the Rev. R. D. Johnston was sent there in 1855. In 1881 the mission was removed to Gooty, where there is now a Training Institution for the Society's Telugu field. In 1890 Anantapur was taken up

In 1893 the Telugu Mission of the London Society had 8 missionaries 880 Church members, 13,252 adherents, and 2,041 scholars.

American Baptist Missionary Union.—The Rev. S. S. Day, the first American Baptist Missionary to the Telugus, landed at Vizagapatam in 1836. The following year he removed to Madras, where he remained three years, preaching both in English and Telugu. In 1840 he removed to Nellore, 108 miles north of Madras, that he might be more among the Telugu people. In 1846, Mr. Day's health required him to visit America. When it was restored, he returned in 1848, accompanied by the Rev. Lyman Jewett and his wife. In 1852 Mr. Jewett baptized for the first time a Telugu.

In 1853 the question was discussed in America, "Shall the Telugu mission be re-inforced or discontinued?" It had been carried on for 17 years with very indifferent success. A proposal was made that a letter should be written to Dr. Jewett requesting him to close the Mission and proceed to Burma. The Secretary said, "Who will write the letter?" giving it to be understood that he would not.

At an evening meeting a speaker, pointing to a mission map on the wall, called Nellore, the "Lone Star Mission," as there was only one station. The Rev. S. F. Smith, author of the American National hymn, caught up the words "lone star," and that night wrote a hymn of which the following are three verses :—

"Shine on, 'Lone Star,' in grief and tears,
And sad reverses oft baptized ;
Shine on amid thy sister spheres :
Lone stars in heaven are not despised.

Shine on "Lone Star!" The day draws near
Where none shall shine more fair than thou ;
Thou, born and nursed in doubt and fear
Will glitter on Immanuel's brow.

Shine on 'Lone Star!' till earth redeemed,
In dust shall bid its idols fall ;
And thousands, where thy radiance beamed,
Shall crown the Saviour, Lord of all."

When this hymn was read, it was unanimously resolved to re-inforce the mission, if it could be done without prejudice to Burma.

During the same year Mr. Day's health again failed, and he had to leave India never to return. It was the custom of the mission to have prayer meetings on the first day of the new year. On the 1st January, 1854, Mr. Jewett was itinerating with his family. The prayer meeting was held on the top of the hill which overlooks Ongole. When it was over, Mr. Jewett, pointing to a piece of rising ground, said, "Would you not like that spot for our mission bungalow and all this land to become Christian? Well, that day will come!" Strange to say, on that piece of ground several years later the mission bungalow was built. The following year Canakiah, afterwards the first ordained pastor of the mission, was baptized.

In 1862 the question was again asked in America, "Shall the Telugu mission be abandoned?" The Secretary pleaded that its settlement should be deferred until the arrival of Mr. Jewett, who was then on his way home. Mr. Jewett told the Committee his determination never to give up the Telugu mission. If the Society declined to aid him, he would go back alone. This was not to be resisted, and it was resolved to send him back, and a new man with him.

In 1864 Mr. Jewett sailed from America, accompanied by the Rev. J. E. Clough. In 1866 the latter settled at Ongole, 182 miles north of Madras, and 10 miles from the Bay of Bengal. In

January following, 28 Madigas, or leather workers, were baptized, and by the close of the year the Ongole church numbered 75 members. The future course of the mission was one of growing prosperity. The year 1869 closed with a total increase of 648. Other labourers came out, and fresh stations were occupied.

The great ingathering at Ongole was after the famine in 1876-77. In addition to the distribution of famine funds all over his field, Mr. Clough took a contract to cut 3½ miles of a canal in order to find employment for his Christians and other poor people in his district. For 15 months those employed were instructed, but none were baptized. When the relief work was over and the labourers were about to leave, such as seemed fit for baptism were accepted. Before the close of the year 9,606 were baptized. The largest number baptized in any one day was 2,222. The membership was thus brought up to 12,804. When the Jubilee of the mission was celebrated in 1886, the number of converts connected with the mission was estimated at 30,000. They have been almost exclusively from the same class of people, the Madigas or leather workers.

A Theological Seminary was established at Ramapatam, 45 miles north of Nellore, in 1872. When Mr. Clough was in America he raised 50,000 dollars as an endowment for the Seminary, and the sum of 15,000 dollars was afterwards obtained for a building. A High School was established at Ongole in 1880, which in 1894 was developed into a College.

In 1894 there were connected with American Baptist Missionary Union 38 foreign missionaries, 54,968 church members, and about 4,000 scholars.

Canadian Baptist Telugu Mission.—Cocanada was occupied by this mission in 1874; Bimlipatam in 1875; Chicacole and Tuni in 1878; Bobbili in 1879; and other stations afterwards. A Theological Seminary was established at Samulcotta in 1882.

In 1893 there were 14 foreign missionaries, about 3,000 communicants, and in the Theological Seminary about 75 students.

C. M. S. Mission.—Bishop Corrie, the first Bishop of Madras, wished the Gospel to be sent to the Telugu country, and after his death £2,000 was raised to open a Mission School at Masulipatam. A request was sent to England in 1840 for men. The letter fell into the hands of Henry Fox of Oxford and Robert Noble of Cambridge. They came out together in 1841. Fox devoted himself to evangelistic work, and Noble to education.

Fox spent six months of the year in a tent passing from village to village, proclaiming the Gospel, sometimes preaching among the Malas and leather workers. When only 30 years of age, he became seriously ill and returned to England, but did not live long. His early death was caused by his devotion to the work, but his dying statement was, "If I had to live over again, I would do the same."

Mr. Noble opened a school at Masulipatam. He began with 2 pupils; but, before long, there was no vacancy. Another teacher was wanted. Mr. Fox, once a Rugby boy under Dr. Arnold, raised a fund among Rugby boys to provide a second master for the School.

Every time that a pupil was baptized, there was a commotion, and some pupils withdrew. The worst outbreak was at the time of the first Brahman conversion. This Brahman, Ratnam, and Bushanam, a high Sudra, broke caste at the same time. They took refuge with Mr. Noble, whose house had to be protected by a guard. The numbers in the School fell from 90 to 4; but it soon recovered, and at each subsequent baptism the excitement diminished. A young Muhammadan, Jani Ali, was one of the early converts. He died in Calcutta in 1894.

In 1864 a terrible hurricane and flood visited Masulipatam. It ravaged the country, and caused the death of at least 35,000 people. Mr. Noble and his pupils were driven to the top room, where the water was up to their knees. Of the boarding school girls 33 were swept away. Their companions heard them pray as they went.

Sickness broke out after the flood. Mr. Noble was urged to go for a change, but he could not make up his mind to leave his post, and he died after a few days' illness. He was a man of great humility. He called himself an "unworthy watchman on the farthest confines of Christ's Church." The people recognized him to be a "holy man," and one of his pupils, who embraced Christianity after his death, said that it was Noble's love that first touched his heart.*

On the 13th November, 1893, the Jubilee of the Masulipatam Noble College was celebrated. It began with 2 boys; at the Jubilee there were upwards of 500 in attendance. The "old boys" bore loving testimony to Mr. Noble's character. "Scarcely less were the encomiums paid to the Rev. J. Sharp, who succeeded Mr. Noble as the Principal of the College." An excellent Female Boarding School, commenced at Masulipatam by Mr. Sharkey, is still maintained. An Institution for the training of mission agents has been added. There are several ladies engaged in zenana work or superintending schools.

It has been mentioned that Mr. Fox itinerated among the villages. This work has been carried on uninterruptedly; several stations have been occupied, and there are thousands of converts. The case of Venkayya, the first convert at Raghavapuram, one of the stations, is interesting. A Hindu friend had heard a Missionary preach about the vanity of idol worship, and the great God, "who dwelleth not in temples made with hands," the "only true God." Venkayya, when told of this, prayed, "*O Great God! Who art Thou! Where art Thou! Show Thyself to me.*"

* C. M. S. *Brief Sketches.*

Three years passed away. Although no preacher came to his village, he heard from others occasionally about a Saviour of sinners. A Christian tract read to him, explained that the great God is Himself the Saviour of a lost world. His prayer then became, "*O great God, the Saviour! show Thyself to me.*" At Bezwada he heard a missionary preach. When he stopped, Venkayya said, "This is my God, this is my Saviour. I have long been seeking for Him; now I have found Him. He is my Saviour, I will serve Him."

Venkayya put himself under instruction, and walked weekly 28 miles to Bezwada. When he returned home, he would tell the people of Raghavapuram what he had learnt; so when the missionary came to baptize him, there were 70 others ready to be baptized.

In 1893 the C. M. S. Telugu Missions had 14 European missionaries, 11,025 Native Christians, 1,812 communicants, and 2,961 scholars.

S. P. G. Mission.—The Telugu Mission of this Society originated at Cuddapah, where a few families separated from the London Society when the Rev. W. Howell joined the Church of England in 1842. The work was formally taken over in 1854, when the Rev. J. Clay became the Society's first Telugu missionary. In 1855 the headquarters were removed from Cuddapah to Mutyalapad, 45 miles to the north. Mr. Clay was joined by the Rev. Messrs. Spencer and Higgins, and systematic work was carried all around. Numbers of Malas, weavers and village labourers, placed themselves under Christian instruction. By 1859 there were 1,146 adherents. In 1861 a new centre was formed at Kalsapad. In 1875 Kurnool was taken up, and in 1883 Nandyal, a new centre where a Training College for native agents was established.

In 1893 there were connected with the Mission 5 European Missionaries, 6,431 Native Christians, 2,117 communicants, and 2,008 scholars.

Godavari Delta Mission.—This mission, which originated with the late Mr. A. N. Groves, was opened by Messrs. W. Bowden and George Beer, who began the mission at Narsapore in 1837. Both died, but they were succeeded by their sons. In 1890 there were 6 European missionaries, (unordained) and 1,000 Native Christians.

American Evan. Lutheran Mission.—In 1842 the Rev. C. F. Heyer commenced a mission at Guntur, which was subsequently placed under the General Synod of the Church. In 1890 there were 5 foreign missionaries and 13,566 Native Christians, with a College at Guntur.

Another mission of the same Church was begun at Rajahmundry by the Rev. Mr. Valett in 1844. In 1890 there were 5 foreign missionaries, and 1,360 Native Christians. Rajahmundry is the chief station. This mission is under the General Council of the Church.

Hermannsburg Ev. Lutheran Mission.—This mission was commenced in 1865 by the Rev. A. Mylius. The Nellore District was selected as the field of labour, to which North Arcot and Cuddapah were afterwards added. In 1890 there were 8 foreign missionaries, and 900 Native Christians.

Wesleyan Mission.—This mission to the Telugus was commenced at Hyderabad in 1880 by the Rev. W. Burgess. Other stations in the Nizam's Dominions were afterwards occupied, with encourag-ing results.

In 1893 there were 6 European missionaries, a Christian community of 3,411, 1,962 full members on trial, and 1,329 scholars connected with the Mission.

THE TAMILS.

The Tamil country extends from Pulicat, 20 miles north of Madras, along the coast to a little beyond Cape Comorin, and inland to the Ghats. Tamil also the language of about one-third of the population of Ceylon. The area of the Tamil country is about 60,000 square miles, nearly the same as that of England and Wales.

Language.—Tamil is the Vernacular of about 15 millions.

TAMIL.

தேவன், தம்முடைய ஒரேபேறான குமாரனை விசுவாசிக்கிறவன் எவனோ அவன் கெட்டுப்போகாமல் நித்திய ஜீவனை அடையும்படிக்கு, அவரைத் தந்தருளி, இவ்வளவாய் உலகத்தில் அன்புகூர்ந்தார்.

Tamil, probably the earliest cultivated of the Dravidian languages, is the most copious, and contains the greatest number of ancient forms.

Although the proportion of Sanskrit in Tamil is less than in the other cultivated Dravidian languages, it amounts to about 40 per cent. The alphabet is supposed to be derived from the early Devanagari, or from the still earlier characters that are contained in the cave inscriptions. The forms are altered by the custom of writing on the leaf of the palmyra palm with an iron stylus.

People.—By an examination of words which are pure Tamil, Bishop Caldwell shows that the Tamils had made some progress in civilization before the southern advance of the Aryans. Agastya is said to have first introduced Sanskrit civilization and literature in the south. He is supposed to have written the first Tamil grammar.

The greatest composition in Tamil is the Kural of Tiruvalluvar, said to have been the work of a poet sprung from the Pariah

TAMIL SCHOOL BOYS.

caste. There is nothing, as an ethical treatise, to equal it in Sanskrit.

Bishop Caldwell says of the Tamils, "Wherever money is to be made, wherever a more apathetic or a more aristocratic people is wishing to be pushed aside, thither swarm the Tamils, the Greeks or Scotch of the east; the least superstitious and the most enterprising and persevering race of Hindus." Throughout Ceylon the coolies on the plantations are Tamils, the majority of the money-making classes in Colombo are Tamils. The majority of the domestic servants of Europeans and of the camp-followers in every part of the Presidency of Madras are Tamils.

As the Mahrattas were the great cave temple excavators, so the Tamils have distinguished themselves by the erection of the largest temples above ground.

Madras has been called "The Benighted," on account of the supposed backward condition of its people. So far as education is concerned, the epithet no longer applies.

Christian Missions.

Protestant missions in India were commenced among the Tamils, and ever since they have received a good deal of attention. A full account has already been given of the early missionaries. The more modern missions will now be described.

Tranquebar Mission.—The narrative given of this mission closes with the death of Schwartz in 1798. He was succeeded at Tanjore by John Caspar Kohlhoff, his adopted son, educated and maintained by him. After this date few missionaries of the Danish Society arrived in India, and although several continued to labour at Tranquebar and elsewhere during the early part of the present century, the interest decreased, and the missions were either abandoned or incorporated with those of other Societies. The remains were afterwards taken up by the Leipzig Mission, which will hereafter be described.

S.P.C.K. and S.P.G. Missions.—The early missions of the Church of England in South India were supported rather by the Christian Knowledge Society than by the Gospel Propagation Society. The assistance also was rather given to the Danish Society than to the Society's own agents. After a time separate missions were formed.

In 1709 the Gospel Society sent £20 and books to Ziegenbalg; and in 1711 the Christian Knowledge Society sent out a printer and press. Schultze came to Madras in 1726, joined the S. P. C. K. two years afterwards, and formed what was called the British Mission of Fort St. George. A small church, consisting of 20 persons, was soon formed, and gradually increased to 400.

Schultze returned to Germany in 1742, when Fabricius took charge, and formed a mission at Vepery, where a printing press was established in 1761. Fabricius died in 1791, when he was 81. He deserves to be long remembered for his version of the Tamil Scripture, and his excellent translations of German hymns. Fabricius was succeeded by Gericke, "the apostolic-minded and premitive Christian." In his days the Vepery Mission flourished.

In 1800 Gericke visited Tinnevelly, and baptized a large number who had been prepared by Satthianadhan, an excellent Native minister ordained by Schwartz. For some years there was no European superintendence of the S. P. G. Mission in Tinnevelly.

In 1825 the S. P. C. K. Missions in South India were transferred to the S. P. G. At the time of the transfer there were 8,352 Christians, and 1,232 scholars, under 6 missionaries. Among the missionaries were the Rev. J. C. Kohlhoff and Dr. Rottler, both far advanced in years. In 1826 what is now the Madras Diocesan Committee was formed. Messrs. Cæmmerer, Heyne, and Kohlhoff, educated at Bishop's College, Calcutta, were sent to Tinnevelly between 1837 and 1839.

The late Bishop Caldwell was born in 1814 near Belfast, and studied at Glasgow. In 1837 he came to India in connection with the London Missionary Society, and laboured at Madras till 1841, where he joined the S. P. G. In 1842, he commenced a station in Tinnevelly at Idaiyangudi, 'the shepherd's home,' where he laboured for nearly 50 years, the work prospering greatly. In 1877, he was consecrated at Calcutta Suffragan Bishop, coadjutor

BISHOP CALDWELL.

to Bishop Gell of Madras. *The Times* says: "His elevation to the episcopate, although an appropriate recognition of his splendid services alike to the Church and to scholarship, brought but little change into his life. He continued as he had been for 40 years, the priest and leader and teacher and organizer of the numerous Christian communities under his care, and a most wise and gentle father and counsellor to the clergy, Indian and European, whose efforts he had long directed, and most of whom had grown up from childhood under his eye. He died in 1891, in his 78th year. Bishop Caldwell wrote in English *The Tinnevelly Shanars, History of Tinnevelly*, and other works; but his *Comparative Grammar of the Dravidian Languages*, is that by which he is most widely known. *The Times* says, "The literary work to which he himself looked back with greatest satisfaction was the part which he took during 11 years in the revision of the Tamil Bible, and when that long labour was ended, in the revision of the Tamil Book of Common Prayer."

The Rev. Henry Bower, formerly of the London Missionary Society, joined the Gospel Society a few months later than Bishop Caldwell. In 1844 he took charge of the Theological Seminary established at Vediarpuram, near Tanjore. He left that station in 1858 for Bible revision work in Madras, on which he was occupied for six years. He was again appointed to missionary work, and was thus engaged till his death in 1885. He wrote several books both in English and Tamil, but his version of the Tamil Bible is his monumental work.

The Rev. Dr. G. U. Pope joined the Mission in 1842. He distinguished himself as a teacher at Sawyerpuram and Tanjore. He has written works which are of great assistance to all students of Tamil, and edited the *Naladiyar*, a noted Tamil poem.

The late Rev. A. R. Symonds was for 26 years the able Principal of the Theological Seminary, in Madras, and Secretary of the Mission. On his retirement, the Institution was placed under the late Rev. Dr. C. E. Kennet, a student of Bishop's College, Calcutta.

In 1893 there were connected with the Tamil Missions of the Society 9 European missionaries, 42,170 Christians, 13,741 communicants, and 15,764 scholars.

London Mission.—The work of this Society among the Tamils was commenced by the Rev. W. T. Ringletaube, an eccentric but earnest missionary. He came out to India in 1804. After spending a year in Madras studying Tamil, he went to Travancore, where he travelled about everywhere preaching. Through the kind offices of Colonel Macaulay, the Resident, he received permission to erect a church at Myladi, on the borders of Tinnevelly. This was the first station of the London Society in the province. Up to 1812, Ringletaube had baptized about 700 persons. In 1816 he left India, and his place was supplied by the Rev. Charles Mead, who made Nagercoil his headquarters. The Seminary at Nagercoil was established in 1819, and a grant of rice fields for its support was obtained from the Rani. The same year the Rev. C. Mault arrived, who was privileged to labour continuously for 35 years in Travancore. In 1838 the mission was strengthened by the arrival of the Rev. James Russell and the Rev. John Abbs. In 1840 there were 15,000 Christians of all ages. Mr. Abbs removed to Parechalay in 1843, and made it the headquarters of a new district. In 1842 the Rev. J. O. Whitehouse took charge of the Seminary at Nagercoil. In 1846 the Rev. E. Lewis arrived from Coimbatore, and in 1853 the

Rev. F. Baylis came from Madras. Both proved very useful labourers. Mr. Baylis devoted much attention to Tamil literature. During 1859, the Rev. J. Duthie arrived from Madras to superintend the Seminary. He has since been privileged to labour continuously in the mission, and is now its senior member. There have been other labourers too numerous to mention. The mission has been favoured with some excellent medical missionaries, as the Rev. C. Leitch who was drowned, and the Rev. J. Lowe. Female education has received a good deal of attention. At Nagercoil there is a very intelligent adult Female Bible Class. The press at Nagercoil has sent forth a large amount of Christian literature. The Seminary in 1893 was affiliated to the Madras University as a Second Grade College. Travancore is the most Brahman ridden state in India. At one ceremony the Maharaja officiates for a short time as one of the bearers of the palanquin of the chief Brahman; he washes his feet and drinks some of the water. Pulayans, a slave caste, were not allowed to approach a Brahman nearer than 96 paces; a Nayar (the highest Sudra) might approach but not touch a Brahman; a palmyra-climber must remain 36 paces off, &c.

At times the Mission has suffered severely from Hindu opposition. Chapels were burned down, Christians assaulted, and the missionaries threatened.

The Rev. W. Loveless arrived in Madras in 1805, but his labours, though useful, were confined to Europeans and East Indians. Work among the Tamils may be said to have commenced with the arrival of the Rev. E. Crisp in 1822. In 1831 there was a Church at Pursewaukum numbering 38 members. The Rev. W. H. Drew joined the mission in 1832, and gave much attention to the native church. In 1852 an English Institution was opened in Black Town, which was maintained till 1894.

The SALEM Mission was commenced in 1827 by the Rev. H. Crisp. In 1840 the Rev. J. M. Lechler joined the Mission. He devoted considerable attention to an Orphan Asylum and School of Industry. In 1870 the Rev. M. Phillips took charge of Salem in addition to Tripatore, to which he was originally appointed.

The Coimbatore Mission was begun in 1830, by the Rev. W. B. Addis, who laboured there for 21 years. Since then there has been a frequent change of missionaries.

The Theological Seminary of the mission is at Bangalore. For some years, till his death in 1894, it was under the Rev. G. O. Newport, a valuable labourer in several departments of missionary work.

In 1893 the Tamil Missions of the Society had 16 European Missionaries, 5,502 Church members, 41,008 adherents, and 17,240 Scholars. The numbers are rather larger, for the Tamil and Malayalam Christians are so mixed at one station that they cannot be separated.

The Church Mission.—The Madras Committee of the C. M. S. was formed in 1814, and shortly afterwards the Rev. Messrs. Rhenius and Schnarré came out from England. Schnarré soon removed to Tranquebar; Rhenius remained till 1820, when he went southward to Tinnevelly. Since then Madras has had a succession of labourers. Besides missionaries engaged in ordinary work, Madras has at times greatly benefited from the Mission Secretaries. Among them may be specially mentioned the Rev. J. Tucker, who exerted a powerful influence for good: "He was surrounded, before long, by a group of laymen, who confessed Christ by mouth and life, and desired to make him known to the heathen."

The mission in Madras occupies now the unique position, in that it is entirely carried on by Natives excepting the special work among Muhammadans, the Divinity Class, and some work among the women. It owed much to the late Rev. W. T. Satthianadhan, B.D., Chairman of the Church Council. He was born of Hindu parents in Madura in 1830, but he was educated at Palamcottah, where he owed his conversion, under God, to Mr. Cruikshanks, a blind teacher of the C. M. S. In 1847 he was baptized by the Rev. John Thomas. While teaching, he married the only daughter of the Rev. J. Devasagayam, the first Native Missionary of the Church of England in South India. For some time he was associated with the North Tinnevelly Itinerants, but in 1861 he was appointed to the Tamil Mission of the C. M. S. in Madras, where he laboured till his lamented death in 1892. Mrs. Satthianadhan, a zealous labourer in the cause of Indian women, was taken away two years before him. Mr. Satthianadhan, during his ministerial career, baptized over 300 converts of all castes. He gave considerable attention to literary work, editing periodicals, and writing books. Among his larger publications may be specially mentioned his Commentary on the New Testament and Church History. It is highly satisfactory that his mantle has fallen upon his children.

The Tinnevelly Mission of the Society originated with the Rev. James Hough, an earnest Chaplain. In 1816, he found 3,000 Native Christians, with a Native Pastor in Tinnevelly. He not only established schools, but studied Tamil that he might write books. On his application to the Church Missionary Society, the Rev. Messrs. Rhenius and Schmid were sent to Tinnevelly in 1820. They had not been long there when whole villages put themselves under Christian instruction. At times the Christians were cruelly persecuted. The work went on prosperously till 1835, when Rhenius seceded from the mission, and about one-third of the Native Christians left with him. Rhenius was unwilling that 6 catechists should be ordained by the Bishop of Madras. He died not very long afterwards, and those who had left returned.

In 1835 a lay agent, Edward Sargent, born in Paris in 1815,

BISHOP SARGENT.

joined the Mission. Two years later the Rev. John Thomas was appointed to Mengnanapuram, which prospered wonderfully under his care. In 1854 the Rev. T. G. Ragland resigned the Madras Secretaryship that he might engage in itinerating work in North Tinnevelly. He was joined by Messrs. Fenn and Meadows and a Native Minister. The Tinnevelly Churches sent catechists for a month at a time, supporting them. When the catechists returned, they described what they had done. The three Cambridge men were sometimes in separate tents, 8 or 10 miles apart, but they all met once a fortnight. Ragland was called away so suddenly in 1858, that he had only time to ejaculate the name of the Saviour.

It has been mentioned that Edward Sargent joined the Mission as a lay agent in 1835. After superintending for some years the Seminary at Palamcottah, he went to England for training and ordination as a missionary. On his return in 1842, he was appointed to Suviseshapuram, where he laboured with success till 1850, when he was transferred to Palamcottah, to take charge of the district, and train candidates for the ministry. On the establishment of the Preparandi Institution two years later, he became its Principal, and retained that post till he was made Bishop Coadjutor to the Bishop of Madras in 1877. About 500 young men passed through the Institution while he was in charge. Under his wise guidance, the Native Church made remarkable progress. When he joined the Mission in 1835, there were 8,693 Christians; when his jubilee was celebrated in 1885, they had increased to 56,287. He visited England in 1888, but he returned to India "to end his days among his own people." He died in 1889.

The Tinnevelly Mission suffered from the withdrawal of too many English missionaries—the number being reduced from 14 to 5. Several have been sent during the last five years, and things are now more hopeful.

The Tinnevelly converts have been chiefly from the Shanars or palmyra climbers. They have been wonderfully raised under Christian influence.

In 1893 there were connected with the Tamil Missions of the Society 13 European missionaries, 55,571 Native Christians, 14,079 communicants, and 19,564 scholars.

Wesleyan Mission.—In 1818 the Rev. J. Lynch was sent over from Ceylon to commence a mission in Madras. In 1821 the Rev. T. H. Squance was stationed at Negapatam. The first Methodist District Meeting ever held in India took place at Negapatam in 1824. The following year the Madras Mission, which up to this time had been connected with Ceylon, was constituted a separate District. The returns up to 1838 show that the missionaries confined their attention almost exclusively to English preaching. During the next decade, though the English causes at Madras and Negapatam were kept up, greater prominence was given to the Native work. In 1839 there were 134 returned as Native members, yet in 1848 the number had fallen to 49. Two Native ministers of long standing joined the Gospel Society, and many of the Native members seceded with them. In 1844 the English Chapel in Black Town was built, and in 1848 the Royapettah property was purchased, the whole cost being raised on the spot by the Rev. Joseph Roberts.

In 1851, it was resolved to establish central institutions to import a superior education to the higher classes of Hindus. These institutions at Madras and Negapatam have worked themselves up to Colleges. About 1853 the Mission was very low as regard European Missionaries. For several years there were only 4 men actually on the ground. In 1855 it was arranged that the Black Town English Church, Madras, should have a pastor who should be exclusively devoted to it. Since that time the greater part of his support has been contributed by the congregation.

Caroor was occupied in 1862. Under the Rev. H. Little the work developed, and a promising industrial institution was added. In the same year, the education of caste girls was commenced in Royapettah, and since then several flourishing girls' schools have been opened at every station.

In 1893 there were connected with the Tamil Mission 14 European missionaries, 1,788 native members or on trial; a Christian community of 3,891, and 6,579 scholars.

American Board.—The Madura Mission of the American Board was commenced in 1836 by the Rev. Messrs. Hoisington and Todd, of the American Jaffna Mission, up to which time no Protestant European missionary, it is believed, had ever resided in the District. The following year 3 other missionaries removed from Jaffna, and an English school was commenced. In 1836 the Rev. Messrs. Poor and Dwight joined the Mission. In 1837 several missionaries came from America. On the arrival of Mr. Poor great attention was paid to vernacular education, and the schools increased until in 1845 the scholars amounted to nearly 4,000. The teachers were heathen. From want of funds and the increase of Christian schools, this system was finally abandoned in 1853. In 1842 a Mission Seminary was established, having for its chief object the raising up of a properly qualified Native agency. In 1843 applications were received from communities in villages to be received as Christians. The desire to escape from oppression was often a motive, but they were brought under instruction, and gradually acquired more knowledge. In 1847 the caste question was forced upon the attention of the mission, and a resolution was passed that no catechist should hereafter be received who did not give satisfactory evidence of having renounced caste. Many of the catechists left, and the Seminary was almost entirely disbanded; but it resulted, in a more healthy state of things, and many afterwards returned.

In 1843 the church members numbered 18, composed almost entirely of the Native agents; in 1875 there were 32 churches, with 1880 members in good standing. The first Native Pastor was ordained in 1855. At first the Native Pastors received their entire support from the Mission; but at present they are supported in whole or in part by the churches over which they have been placed, and in part by the Native Evangelical Society.

The Pasumalei Seminary, near Madura, has contributed greatly to the success of the Mission. It has had the benefit of two missionaries, each privileged to labour in connection with it for many years—the Rev. Drs. Tracy and Washburn. A Home deputation discouraged for a time English education; but the Seminary has now developed into an English College. In addition there is a Training School for teachers and a Theological class. In Madura there is an excellent Girls' Boarding School.

The Rev. Dr. Chester, besides acting as missionary physician, has for many years superintended hospitals and dispensaries. In 1886 a women's dispensary was established at Madura under a lady doctor.

In 1893 there were connected with the Mission 14 Foreign missionaries, 14,810 adherents and communicants, 4,109 communicants, and 6,873 scholars.

Free Church of Scotland Mission.—The eloquent appeals of Dr. Duff in Scotland for India, led the Rev. John Anderson to offer himself to the Church of Scotland as a missionary. He landed in India in 1836. Shortly before his arrival the Scottish chaplains of Madras had founded what was called St. Andrew's School. This was placed under Mr. Anderson's care, who issued a circular stating that the school would be thoroughly Christian. Before the close of 1838, the attendance had increased from 59 to 277.

Two pariah boys had found their way into the school under false colours. When discovered their expulsion was demanded. As this request could not be complied with, about 100 of the pupils left the school; but in a few months their places were filled up.

Early in 1839 Mr. Anderson was cheered by the arrival of a second missionary, the Rev. R. Johnston. A few months later a school was opened at Conjevaram, a great Hindu centre; shortly afterwards, another was set up at Chingleput. In 1841 Mr. and Mrs. Braidwood arrived. The efforts of both were early directed to female education.

The first student to express a wish to become a Christian was a Telugu youth, named Ettirajulu; but before he was received P. Rajahgopal and A. Venkataramiah were baptized. When Rajahgopal applied for baptism, Mr. Anderson asked if he was prepared to give up his mother, his sisters, and his all for Christ. On his replying that he was, "Well," said Mr. Anderson, "I am prepared to give up my school for you." When it was known that the two had applied for baptism, the mission house was besieged by their relatives, and it was represented to the chief magistrate that the youths were forcibly detained. Mr. Anderson then took them to the Police Court, where they said they wished to go with him, and were permitted to do as they said. Both were baptized by Mr. Anderson in June, 1841. Ettirajulu had been confined at home, but at last he managed to make his escape, and arrived at the mission house, with the marks of the scourge upon his face. He was baptized in August of the same year.

The Institution and branch schools suffered severely for a time in consequence of these baptisms: about 400 left, and only 30 or 40 remained. But Mr. Anderson said, "A school ceases to be missionary if men shrink from the thing they have been seeking and desiring, and the Churches of Christ have been praying for."

To reach the young men thus scattered, Mr. Anderson commenced a fortnightly periodical, called the *Madras Native Herald*, which was carried on for many years.

The Institution was not long in recovering from the shocks it had received. When the next annual examination took place, the number present was nearly as large as before, and the Chief Justice, who presided, defended the missionaries from the charge of having in any way dealt unfairly with the pupils in aiming at their conversion. At the examination in 1843, the chair was occupied by the Governor, the Marquis of Tweeddale.

In 1843 the three Scottish Madras Missionaries left the Church of Scotland, and joined the Free Church. Space does not permit the future history of the mission to be described in detail. Nearly every year till Mr. Anderson's death in 1855, there were converts from the Institution. The appeals of Mr. Anderson to the students to accept the gospel message were most fervid.

For a few years after the death of Mr. Anderson, the work was fairly maintained; but from the many changes and reduction in the number of labourers, it gradually fell very low. In 1862, when things were at the worst, the Rev. W. Miller, joined the

REV. DR. W. MILLER.

Mission, and soon a change took place. The Institution was gradually developed into a First Grade College, with a large staff of professors, while the attendance in the College Classes rose to about 800, besides 1000 in the School Department. For his services in connection with the Education Commission, Mr. Miller was made a C. I. E. in 1884. The College buildings have been greatly enlarged through Dr. Miller's liberality. Besides additional classrooms, hostels have been erected for the accommodation of various classes of students. It may be said of him, *Si monumentum requiris, circumspice.**

It has been mentioned Mr. and Mrs. Braidwood commenced female education in Madras. They began in September, 1843, with only 5 pupils. In May 1844 there were 24 in attendance, which was thought 'an encouraging number.' The work has been maintained ever since with increasing success. There are Female Normal Schools, a large Boarding School, and a number of day schools, besides Zenana and Medical work.

At Chingleput, south of Madras, there is promising village work under the Rev. A. Andrew.

In 1893 there were 8 European ordained missionaries connected with the Mission, 442 communicants and 841 baptized adherents. The College and schools contained 3,644 pupils.

Church of Scotland Mission.—When Mr. Anderson and his two brethren joined the Free Church in 1843, the Church of Scotland sent out other missionaries. The Institution has been maintained as a Second Grade College, and evangelistic work has been carried on both in Madras and at outstations. Considerable attention has also been paid to female education and other efforts among the women.

In 1893 there was one European ordained missionary, with 149 communicants and 560 baptized adherents. There were 2,227 pupils in schools and zenanas.

Leipzig Evan. Luth. Mission.—In 1840 this Society sent out the Rev. H. Cordes as its first missionary to India. He began his labours at Tranquebar in connection with the Danish Mission. The Rev. C. Ochs arrived in 1842, and the Rev. J. M. N. Schwarz the following year. In 1849 the Danish Mission, with about 1,200 Christians and all its property, was transferred to the Leipzig Society. More labourers were sent out in the course of time, and the work extended. At Tranquebar there is a Seminary, an Industrial School, and a Mission Press.

The mission differs in allowing greater latitude to caste than in other missions.

In 1893 there were connected with the Mission 30 European missionaries, 14,130 Native Christians, 6,886 communicants, and 4,827 scholars.

---

* If you seek my monument, look around.

American Arcot Mission.—In 1851, the Rev. H. M. Scudder, who had already been labouring for some years in Madras as a missionary of the American Board, obtained leave to seek a new field of labour. Selecting the Arcot District, he established a Medical Dispensary at Wallajanagar. The following year he was joined by his two brothers, the Rev. Messrs. W. W. and Joseph Scudder. In 1853 they were constituted a new mission, under the name of the "American Arcot Mission of the Reformed Protestant Dutch Church of America." The mission had then only 8 communicants and a small school for the children of Church members. In 1857 an amicable separation was made from the American Board, since which the Mission has been directly responsible to the Home Church. Since that period there has been steady growth. The work has been extended to South Arcot, and parts of Cuddapah and Mysore.

In 1892 there were 9 Foreign ordained missionaries, 1,881 communicants, and 6,504 Christian adherents. The schools contained 4,517 children.

Danish Mission.—This mission was commenced in 1865 by the Rev. C. Ochs. The first station was Pattambakam, near Cuddalore. About 1869 the Rev. P. Anderson took up Tirukoilur. Other stations, including Madras, were afterwards occupied.

In 1893 there were 7 foreign missionaries connected with the Society; 636 Native Christians, 247 communicants, and 357 scholars.

CANARESE.

Canarese, properly Kanadi or Karnatika, is spoken throughout the table-land of Mysore, and northward as far as Beder in the Nizam's Territory. It is also the prevailing language in Canara on the Western Coast. The area may be roughly estimated at 65,000 square miles.

CANARESE.

ಯಾಕಂದರೆ ಅವನಲ್ಲಿ ವಿಶ್ವಾಸವಿಡುವವರೆಲ್ಲರು ನಾಶವಾಗದೆ, ನಿತ್ಯಜೀವ
ವನ್ನು ಹೊಂದುವ ಬಗ್ಗೆ, ದೇವರು ಒಬ್ಬನಾಗಿ ಹುಟ್ಟಿದ ತನ್ನ ಮಗನನ್ನು
ಕೊಡುವಹಾಗೆ, ಲೋಕವನ್ನು ಅಷ್ಟು ಪ್ರೀತಿ ಮಾಡಿದನು.

Language.—Canarese is spoken by about 9 millions. The alphabet is nearly the same as the Telugu. The language includes two dialects—ancient and modern—differing in their use of inflexional terminations. All really ancient inscriptions in the Hala Kannada or ancient Canarese character, are in Sanskrit.

People.—The Canarese are an agricultural people. Ragi is their chief food. In disposition they are conservative. The kingdom of the mythical Sugriva, whose general, Hanuman, aided Rama, was in the Canarese country. Vijayanagar, was a great Hindu kingdom from 1118 to 1565 A.D. Vast ruins of temples, fortifications, tanks and bridges, belonging to its capital, can still be traced on the right bank of the Tungabhadra river. Last century Hyder Ali made Mysore, for a time, a powerful state.

Religion.—Jainism prevailed in the Canarese country for several centuries towards the early part of the Christian era. In the Hassan District of Mysore there is a small town famous for its colossal image of the Tirthankar Gomatesvara. The statue is 56½ feet high, cut out of one solid block of stone. It stands on the top of a rocky hill, and can be seen for miles. The Jains say that Rishaba, their first Tirthankar, was 500 poles, about 1½ miles high! Mahavira, the 24th, degenerated to the size of a man. The statue is naked, so its maker must have belonged to the Svetambara, or sky-clad sect. Once in 20 years, the great ceremony of washing the image is performed.

The Canarese country is noted as containing the largest number of Lingaites, also called Vira-Saivas. They are a subdivision of the Saivas, worshipping only the male energy. The other Saivas associate the yoni with the linga. They are distinguished by wearing a small linga, enclosed in a metal case. Hence they are called *Lingadharis*. Sometimes they are called *Jangamas*, from *jangama*, motion, claiming to be living symbols of the deity. The mendicants often lead about a bull, a type of the bull of Siva. *Vira* is derived from a word meaning bravery. They nearly exterminated the Jains in some parts of the Dekkan.

CHRISTIAN MISSIONS.

London Mission.—The London Society commenced Protestant Missions among the Canarese. In 1810 the Rev. John Hands settled at BELLARY, where he laboured continuously for 18 years. In 1816 the Rev. W. Reeve joined the Mission, and in 1819 the first native member was received into the church. In 1826 Mr. Price was sent out from England to take charge of the press recently set up. For several years it was the only press then existing for the printing of Christian publications in Canarese and Telugu. The following year the devoted and zealous Native preacher, Samuel Flavel, joined the Mission, and laboured successfully till his death in 1847. In 1828 Mr. Hands left for England. Besides preaching, he established the first Tract Society in India, and translated nearly the whole Bible into Canarese. In 1830 the Rev. John Reid arrived at Bellary, where he laboured till his death in 1841. The following year the Rev. J. S. Wardlaw joined the Mission. About 1846 he founded an institution which has developed into the Wardlaw College.

The BELGAUM Mission of the London Society was commenced in 1820 by the Rev. Joseph Taylor, sent from Bellary. In 1828 he was joined by the Rev. W. Beynon. Both were privileged to labour for many years at Belgaum. This station has had comparatively few changes of labourers.

The BANGALORE Mission was commenced in 1820 by the Rev. S. Laidler. The first chapel was erected a year after his arrival, in which he preached to an English congregation. A Tamil congregation was collected in the same chapel by the zealous native evangelist, Samuel Flavel, who was ordained pastor in 1822, and continued till 1827, when he was removed to Bellary. A Canarese congregation was gathered by the Rev. W. Campbell about the year 1827. About the same time a Canarese Boarding School and Theological Seminary were commenced. In 1835 the Rev. C. Campbell joined the Mission, with which he was connected till 1875, when he retired. Street preaching and itineration were his chief work. The Rev. B. Rice arrived in 1836, and continued to labour till his death in 1887. He was engaged in all branches of missionary work. He was one of the revisors of the Canarese Bible; Secretary of the Bangalore Bible and Tract Societies, the author or translator of a number of books and tracts in Canarese and English. During 51 years he went only once on furlough. In 1840 Mrs. Sewell succeeded in establishing the first Canarese girls' day school. In 1849 an Anglo-Canarese Theological Seminary was begun under the Rev. J. Sewell. The English Institution was commenced by the Rev. B. Rice in 1858. The Rev. J. B. Coles, who laboured for many years in different parts of the Canarese country, died at Bangalore in 1891. In the Canarese Mission a number of the converts have been Tamils.

In 1893 there were connected with the Mission, 10 European missionaries, 353 church members, 940 adherents, and 3,734 scholars.

Wesleyan Mission.—In 1820 the Rev. Elijah Hoole and the Rev. James Mowat were appointed to labour in Mysore. They made Bangalore their headquarters, but their efforts were confined to Europeans and Tamils. In 1833 the Rev. T. Hodson came from Calcutta to commence work among the Canarese people. In 1835 he erected a building for an English school, which now forms part of the Native Educational Institution: In 1836 he made a tour through the country to select new stations. Gubbi was chosen in 1837, and soon after the city of Mysore, Kunigal, and Tumkur were occupied. During 1839 the Rev. W. Arthur arrived from England, but he was obliged to leave through sickness in 18 months. In 1840 a Mission Press was established, the first set up in the Mysore Province. Under the supervision of the missionaries, 4 founts of superior types were afterwards prepared. In 1843 the Rev. M. T. Male baptized at Gubbi a man and his 3 sons, the first fruits among the Canarese. In 1853 a petition was received for the establishment of an English school at Mysore. It was commenced in 1854 by the Rev. E. T. Hardey, and has been maintained ever since. In 1861 three young men belonging to a suburb of Mysore were baptized by the Rev. J. Hutcheon. In 1860 Shimoga was opened as a mission station by the Rev. J. S. Banks. In 1872 the Mission Press was sold. Among the works issued from it may be specially mentioned the first edition of the Canarese Bible in one volume, and the Canarese and English Dictionary of the Rev. D. Sanderson. In 1878 the Rev. T. Hodson, the founder of the Wesleyan Canarese Mission, returned to England. He was succeeded as Chairman of the District by the Rev. Josiah Hudson.

In 1893 the number of English missionaries was 11; Canarese church members 948; day scholars, 8,450. There were also 573 Tamil and English church members.

Basel Mission.—In 1833, when, on the renewal of the East India Company's Charter, India was opened to settlers from foreign countries, the Basel Missionary Society at once resolved to establish a mission there. In 1834 three missionaries, the Rev. Messrs. Hebich, Lehner, and Greiner arrived at Mangalore in South Canara, on the Western Coast. The first converts of the mission was baptized at Mangalore in 1837, and in the same year Dharwar, in the Southern Mahratta country, was occupied. At the close of 1840, the church consisted of 8 communicants. In 1843 Mulky, 20 miles north of Mangalore, was taken up. Honavar, in North Canara, was afterwards made a station.

The educational work of the Mission includes purely Christian schools, catechist seminaries, elementary vernacular schools for heathen or mixed schools, Anglo-vernacular and high schools.

In 1841 a lithographic press was established at Mangalore, to which typographic presses were afterwards added. The Mission Press is now a large establishment, with work inferior to none in India. In 1850 two laybrethren arrived to teach the converts new trades. Watch and clockmaking were commenced, but they were found unsuitable. In 1851 a laybrother arrived to introduce European improvements in weaving. This has been very successful. 1854 another laybrother came out thoroughly acquainted with mercantile affairs to take charge of the industrial undertakings and of the mission treasury. A shop was also set up which flourishes under his care.

The industrial and mercantile establishments are a characteristic feature of the mission, but they are worked by separate funds, and managed by a separate committee. In 1890 there were connected with the mission (including the Malayalam work) 6 weaving establishments, 4 tile factories, one mechanical establishment and one carpentry. The work in each is begun daily by scripture reading, exposition, and prayer. In connection with the Press there is a thoroughly organized system of sub-depôts, and a staff of 12 colporteurs.

In 1893 there were connected with the Canarese stations 46 European agents, 3,580 communicants, 3,395 children and catechumens, and 3,683 scholars.

Other Mission.—The Gospel Society has long had small missions in the Mysore Province; the Leipzig Society has also had a mission at Bangalore since 1873, but the work of both has been among Tamils. The American Episcopal Methodists formerly laboured only among the English-speaking community, but lately a private Canarese mission at Kolar has been taken over.

NILGIRI TRIBES.

The Nilgiri Hills, to the south of Mysore, are inhabited by several tribes.

The TODAS, properly Tudas, were not the original inhabitants, although the other hill tribes acknowledge them to be their superiors. There are graves of raised blocks of unhewn stone of which the Todas know nothing.

The Todas are a fine, well-proportioned, powerful people, with large and sometimes aquiline nose. They are nevertheless indolent,

TODAS.

and disinclined to work of every description. Their sole labour is watching their cattle, milking the kine, and manufacturing ghi. Their bodies are enwrapped in one long garment, their heads are uncovered; their hair both of head and beard is uncut; they are copper-coloured in complexion. The women decorate themselves with massive necklaces, and wear their hair flowing over their shoulders, though sometimes it is curled up with short sticks. They tattoo, with black dye, their necks, hands and lips in imitation of jewelry.

The language of the Todas was originally old Canarese; but it is now more allied to Tamil than to any other dialect. They never wash their clothes and seldom their bodies, from their birth to their death. The roofs and sides of their huts are formed of twisted bamboos. The end wall is strongly built; the front wall has an opening so small that those who enter must crawl on their hands and feet.

The Todas all practise polyandry, one woman being the wife of all the brothers of a family, with each of whom she lives a month at a time. Formerly when the tribe was not under the British, only one female child was allowed to survive in each household.

The Todas are greatly attached to their buffaloes. On returning from the fields in the evening, these animals are saluted with much respect by their masters.

An attempt was made to get some of the children to go to school; but they would not learn.

Four other tribes inhabit the Nilgiri Hills—the Badagas, Kotas, Kurumbas, and Irulas.

The BADAGAS, northmen, are supposed to have come from the north on account of famine and persecution about 300 years ago. Their language is an old Canarese dialect. They are the most numerous, wealthy and civilised of the indigenous tribes. In 1881 they numbered 24,000; they pay tribute to the Todas.

The KOTAS are filthy in their habits and much addicted to eating carrion. They perform menial offices for the Todas and Badagas, &c.

The KURUMBAS (shepherds) collect jungle products, &c. All the other tribes stand in awe of them, and some of them officiate as priests to the Badagas.

The IRULAS from (*irul*, darkness) live on the lowest slopes. They use animal food of every description, and are expert huntsmen.

Basel Mission.—Mr. Casamajor left a legacy to the Basel Mission to enable a mission to the Nilgiris to be commenced. It was opened in 1846. Canarese and Badaga are the languages chiefly used. Tamil is taught in the schools. Several Badagas have been baptized, although at times they have been exposed to severe persecution.

In 1893 there were connected with the Mission 5 Foreign missionaries, 412 Christians including 189 communicants, and 685 scholars.

TULUS.

Tulu is a Dravidian dialect, spoken by nearly half a million on the west coast of India, around Mangalore, about midway between Bombay and Cape Comorin. It is destitute of a literature in the proper sense of the term, and never had a character of its own. The Canarese character having been used by the missionaries in the Tulu books printed by them at Mangalore—the only books ever printed in Tulu,—that character has now become associated with the language. Notwithstanding this, Tulu is one of the most highly developed languages of the Dravidian family. It differs most widely from Tamil, and least from Canarese. All Tulu Christians are taught Canarese as well as Tulu. Tulu, however, shows no signs of disappearing, and the people have the reputation of being the most conservative portion of the Dravidian race. The name Tulu is said to mean mild, humble.

Basel Mission.—This Society has 7 stations in which mission work on the West Coast is carried on in Tulu and Canarese. The two are so mixed up that they cannot be separated. Tulu Christians are included among the Canarese.

MALAYALIS.

Malayalam is an ancient offshoot of Tamil, though now a good deal altered. It is spoken along the south-west coast of India, from near Trevandrum to Chandragiri, near Mangalore. The name means "mountain region." In Sanskrit the country is called Kerala.

The country consists chiefly of hills and dales, intersected by streams running from east to west, and forming large back-waters connected with the sea. These, not roads, form the great medium of communication between the districts. The village system is little known, and the inhabitants live, each in his own palm garden, along the banks of the rivers and paddy lands.

Calicut, in the Malayalam country, was the first port in India where the Portuguese landed in 1498.

Language.—Malayalam is spoken by about 5½ millions. It differs from Tamil chiefly at present by its disuse of the personal terminations of the verb, and the larger proportion of Sanskrit derivatives, which is greatest in Malayalam of the Dravidian languages. The modern character is derived mainly from the Grantha, the character in which Sanskrit is written in the Tamil country.

MALAYALAM.

എന്തുകൊണ്ടെന്നാൽ ദൈവം തന്റെ ഏകജാതനായ പുത്രനെ, അ
വനിൽ വിശ്വസിക്കുന്നവൻ ഒരുത്തനും നശിച്ചു പോകാതെ, നിത്യ
ജീവൻ ഉണ്ടാകേണ്ടുന്നതിനു, തരുവാൻ തക്കവണ്ണം എത്രയും ലോക
ത്തെ സ്നേഹിച്ചു.

A dialect of Malayalam is spoken by the Muhammadans on the Malabar Coast, called Mappilas or Moplas, and by the inhabitants of the Laccadive Islands. An adaptation of the Arabic alphabet is used.

People.—Travancore, forming the south of the Malayalam country, is well called by the Brahmans *Dharma Bhumi*, the Land of Charity, for in no other part of India is so much money spent on feeding them. At one ceremony the Maharaja officiates for a short time as one of the bearers of the palanquin of the chief Brahman; he washes his feet and drinks some of the sacred water. He is a Sudra, but he is made a twice-born by passing through a golden cow or lotus. The cow is of the same weight as himself, and is afterwards distributed among the Brahmans. The Maharaja, thenceforward, cannot eat with the members of his family, but he is admitted to the high privilege of seeing the Brahmans enjoying their meals, and of eating in their presence.

The Sudras are the middle classes in Travancore. The greater portion of the land is in their hands, and, until recently, they were the principal owners of slaves. They are usually called

MALAYALAM LADY.

Nayars, lords or masters. Their customs with regard to marriage are singular. A girl is nominally married in early youth, but it is a mere formality. When arrived at a marriageable age, she accepts any suit as she pleases, but the engagement is not binding on either party, and can be easily dissolved. Hence the children of a Sudra family inherit the property, not of their father, but of their mother's brother. The custom of polyandry, or one woman having several husbands, is sometimes practised.

Pulayans, a slave caste, were not allowed to approach a Brahman nearer than 96 paces; a Nayar might approach but not touch a Brahman; a palmyra-climber must remain 36 paces off. Education is spreading in Travancore, and by degrees, it is hoped, caste distinctions will disappear.

The bulk of the Malayalam people are Hindus; but Christians are more numerous than in any other part of India. An account has already been given of the Syrian Christians. Protestant Missions will now be described.

MISSIONS.

Church Mission.—As already mentioned, this mission was commenced in 1816 by the Rev. Messrs. Bailey, Baker and Fenn. No proselytes were made, an internal reform of the Syrian Church being attempted. When this failed through the hostility of the authorities of the Syrian Church, in 1837 a separation took place. From that time the Mission began to make converts from the heathen and to receive Syrians. Several stations were at once established. One was at Cottayam in charge of Mr. Bailey; another was in the neighbourhood, superintended by Mr. Baker; a third was at Mavelikara, under Mr. Peet. Trichur, in the Cochin State, was occupied in 1841. Gradually other stations were formed both in Travancore and Cochin. In 1869 a Church Council was formed, and in 1879 the Rev. J. M. Speechly was consecrated the first Bishop of Travancore.

At Cottayam, the headquarters of the Mission, there is a College, a Divinity School, and a Printing Press.

The late Rev. H. Baker laboured with much success among the Hill Arrians, of whom there are now about 3,000 Christians. They thus appealed to him, "We die like beasts, and are buried like dogs; ought you to neglect us?" Many Pulayans have embraced Christianity. There have been a few Brahman converts.

In 1893 the statistics of the Mission were as follows: European missionaries 12; Native Christians 29,594; communicants, 8,628; scholars 8,107.

London Mission.—The Malayalam Mission of this Society was commenced at Quilon in 1821 by the Rev. John Smith. Trevandrum was not then open to missionary effort on account of the Brahman dread of pollution by Europeans and Native Christians.

In 1838, through the influence of General Frazer, the Resident, the opposition was withdrawn, and the Rev. John Cox commenced the mission. The Raja gave a site for buildings, and Mr. Cox found 40 Christians already on the spot. Here Mr. Cox laboured for 23 years, and notwithstanding cruel persecutions from the Government officials and others, the converts rose from 40 to 1511. Trevandrum is of special importance as containing the Maharaja's College, which is numerously attended.

In 1893 there were connected with the Mission 4 European missionaries, 1,824 church members, 13,491 adherents, and 3,433 scholars.

Basel Mission.—This Mission occupies the northern part of the Malayalam country. Its work was commenced in Malabar in 1839, in which there are now 7 stations, the principal of which are Cannanore, Tellicherry, Calicut, and Codacal. There are weaving establishments and tile works at several places. Near Tellicherry there is a Theological Seminary, besides a Christian High School, and Training Institution. There are also several orphanages.

In 1893 the statistics of the Mission were as follows: European Brethren, 24; communicants, 2,222; children of communicants, 1,971; scholars, 2,817.

ZENANA MISSIONS.

The origin of these has been described (page 37), and there are occasional notices of their work; but they have not received sufficient attention. This has arisen partly from want of space, but chiefly from the want of sufficient details. In several cases no information whatever was available. Should another edition of this sketch be issued, it is hoped that something will be done to remedy the omission.

BIBLE TRANSLATIONS AND SOCIETIES.

These have been noticed incidentally, but a brief general view may be given. As in the case of missions, only the early efforts and the principal languages can be described. The information is abridged from *Biblical Translations in India*, by Mrs. Macleod Wylie, of Calcutta, published in 1854.

Tamil.—The earliest attempt at translating the Scriptures into an Indian language was made by the Dutch in Ceylon. In 1688 the translation of the New Testament into Tamil was commenced, and in 1694 that of the Old Testament. The work, however was not carried on regularly. The translation of the whole Bible by the early Danish missionaries has been described.

Telugu.—This was the second Indian language into which part of the Scriptures was translated. In 1727, Schultze finished a translation of the New Testament. The MS. was sent to Halle, but never printed. A translation was commenced by Messrs. Cran and Des Granges, sent out to Vizagapatam in 1804. Their translation of Luke was printed in 1810; the other three Gospels were published the following year. In 1814 Mr. Pritchett completed the translation of the New Testament. This was accepted by the Calcutta Bible Society, and printed at Madras in 1819. Mr. Pritchett was engaged on the translation of the Old Testament when he died. The work was afterwards taken up by Mr. Gordon. The late Dr. John Hay did much for the improvement of the Telugu Scriptures.

Hindustani or **Urdu.**—This was the third Indian language into which part of the Scriptures was translated. The Danish missionaries translated the Psalms into South Indian Hindustani, sometimes called Dekkani, and they were printed at Halle in 1747. In 1804 an edition of the Gospels in Northern Hindustani was issued from the College Press of Fort William. It was translated by Dr. W. Hunter, and was printed in the Nagri character. In 1805 Henry Martyn arrived in Calcutta, and immediately commenced studying Hindustani with a view to the translation of the Scriptures. He was assisted by Mirza Fitrut, an eminent Hindustani scholar, and in 1808 his translation of the New Testament was finished. It was sent to press at Serampore in 1811, but from the fire in 1812, it was not completed till 1815. In 1819 a commencement was made in translating the Old Testament. In 1828 the first volume was published, and in 1842 it was completed. The revision of the Urdu Scriptures is being continued till the present day.

Bengali.—Before 1791 Mr. Thomas had translated several portions of Scriptures, which were circulated in manuscript. In 1794 Carey began the study of Bengali. In 1797 the translation of the New Testament was completed; in 1801 the first edition was printed. The translation of the Old Testament was finished in 1800; in 1809 the whole Bible was printed in 5 large volumes. The labours of Drs. Yates and Wenger for the improvement of the version have been noticed.

Sanskrit.—Carey commenced the study of Sanskrit soon after he came to India. In 1806 his translation of the New Testament was sent to press, and in 1809 the printing was completed. In 1811 the Pentateuch was printed, and in 1818 the Sanskrit Scriptures were finished. As in the case of Bengali, Drs. Yates and Wenger did much for Sanskrit revision.

Serampore Versions.—A statement has been given of what the Serampore missionaries proposed and accomplished under the head of Bible translations. The specimen page below was issued, giving a list of some of the language. The type has since been greatly improved.

FAC-SIMILE OF THE TEXT, "The people which sat in darkness saw great light" (Matt. iv. 16), in the following Eastern languages:—

1. Bengalee.
2. Orissa.
3. Hindoostanee, or Urdu.
4. Sanscrit.
5. Telinga, or Telegu.
6. Kurnata.
7. Afghan.
8. Burman.
9. Tamil.
10. Cingalese.
11. Malay.
12. Chinese.

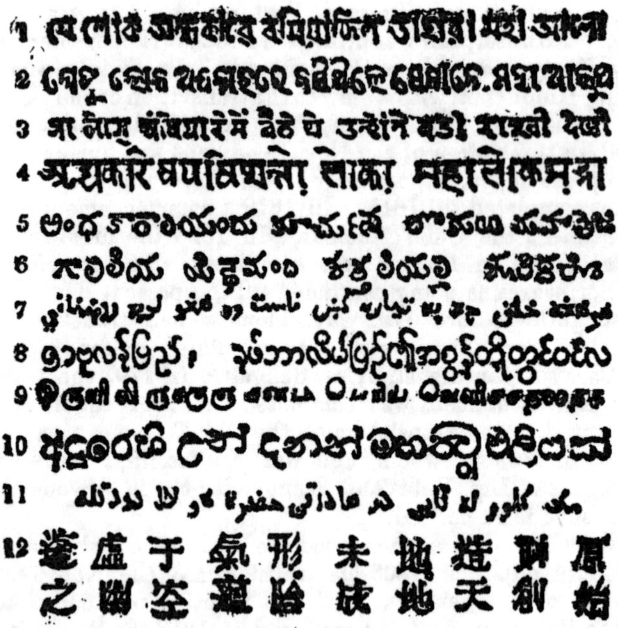

Marathi.—Carey engaged a pandit to translate the New Testament into this language. After revision, the New Testament was completed in 1805. In 1815 the Pentateuch was printed at Serampore, and in 1819, the Old Testament was completed. After missions were commenced in Western India, improved versions of the Scriptures were issued.

Hindi.—In 1803 Carey commenced the translation of the New Testament in what was supposed to be Hindi, but it was found more to resemble Hindustani. In 1811 it was printed, and in 1818 the Serampore version of the Old Testament was issued. In 1818, Mr. Bowley began a Hindi version and by the following year the four Gospels were printed. His translation was much admired. Chamberlain's translation of the New Testament was finished in 1820, but the printing was delayed. Mr. Bowley's translation of the New Testament was completed in 1823; his Old Testament was finished in 1836. Since then several editions of the Hindi Scriptures have been printed both in Nagri and Kaithi. The revision is still in progress.

Malayalam.—Dr. Buchanan visited South India in 1806 to obtain information about the Syrian Christians. Besides taking measures for the publication of the Scriptures in Syriac, he sought also to have them issued in Malayalam. In 1807 arrangements were made for the translation being carried on by Mar Dionysius, the Syrian Metropolitan, and three assistants, under the superintendence of Colonel Macaulay, the Resident. The translation of the Gospels was sent to Calcutta the same year, but they could not be printed from the want of Malayalam types. The printing was executed at Bombay a year or two later. On the establishment of the Church Mission, it was resolved to translate anew the whole Scriptures and print them at Cottayam. Mr. Bailey was specially devoted to this work. Mr. Spring, a chaplain, also prepared a version of nearly the whole of the New Testament. In 1829 the printing of the New Testament was completed; and in 1841 the Old Testament. Another version was afterwards prepared by the Basel Mission. A joint version is now in progress.

Oriya.—The translation of the New Testament in this language was commenced in 1804, and it was printed at Serampore in 1809. In 1811, the poetical and prophetical books of the Old Testament were published; in 1814 the historical books; in 1815 the Pentateuch, and thus the Oriya Scriptures were completed. Revised translations were afterwards published.

Assamese.—A translation in Assamese was commenced at Serampore in 1810. The New Testament was printed in 1819, the Pentateuch in 1822, and the whole Bible in 1832. Revised editions were prepared after the establishment of Missions in Assam. The Rev. N. Brown distinguished himself as a translator.

Canarese.—In 1809 the Serampore missionaries had translated the New Testament into Canarese, but from want of funds it was not printed till 1817. In 1809 the Rev. John Hands was sent out to the Canarese country. In 1817 he wrote that the whole of the New Testament had been translated. In 1820 the Gospels and Acts were printed from his translation. Mr. Reeve undertook the historical books of the Old Testament, and Mr. Hands the Psalms and Prophets. In 1827 the Pentateuch was ready, and other books followed. The printing of the Old Testament was completed in 1831. The Canarese translation is now being revised.

Gujurati.—The Serampore missionaries printed the New Testament in what was supposed to be Gujarati, but this was found not to be the case. In 1815 Messrs. Skinner and Fyvie arrived at Surat. By the end of 1817 they had translated the New Testament and the Pentateuch into Gujarati. In 1821 the whole of the New Testament was printed, and the Old Testament was completed in 1823. Revised editions were afterwards issued.

Punjabi.—The Serampore missionaries issued the New Testament in 1815; the Pentateuch in 1817, and the whole Scriptures in 1826. In 1834 the American Presbyterian Mission was established at Ludhiana, and in 1837 the Rev. John Newton commenced a new translation. Mr. Newton was privileged to labour for upwards of fifty years in the Punjab, and did much to improve the translation of the Punjabi Scriptures.

Bible Societies.

Only a brief tabular statement can be given :—

When formed.		Subscriptions. Rs.	Sales. Rs.	Issues. 1893.
1810	Calcutta Auxiliary ...	1,968	6,234	124,691
1820	Madras Auxiliary ...	16,458*	6,795	157,689
1813	Bombay Auxiliary ...	1,407	3,905	62,741
......	North India ...	1,810	8,455	72,750
1837	Bangalore ...	......	......	9,537
1863	Punjab ...	353	4,627	45,740
				473,148

The following is a list of the Scriptures in the languages of India printed or purchased for the British and Foreign Bible Society up to March, 1894 :†

Assamese ...	300	Hindustani (Madras) ...	123,080
Badaga ...	2,000	Indo-Portuguese ...	18,000
Bengali ...	1,561,260	Kashmiri ...	18,600
Do. Mussulman ...	135,060	Khasi ...	35,372
Canarese ...	439,000	Khondi ...	1,000
Chamba (Takri) ...	3,512	Koi ...	2,526
Gond ...	1,500	Konkani ...	4,000
Gujarati ...	214,127	Kutchi ...	500
Hindi (Kaithi) ...	343,800	Lepcha ...	2,000
—— (Nagri) ...	977,945	Magadhi ..	2,000
Hindustani Roman ...	153,917	Malayalam ...	675,365
———— Nagri ...	7,000	Marathi ...	596,597
———— (Arabic) ...	257,699	——— (Modi) ...	82,030
———— (Persian) ...	585,412	Marwari ...	1,000

* Sales at out-station Depôts are included.

† Report of the British and Foreign Bible Society.

Mundari (Kol)	...	38,570	Santali	...	43,066
Nepali	...	26,000	Sindhi	...	65,247
Oriya	...	40,000	Tamil	...	3,009,150
Pali	...	500	Telugu	...	1,231,300
Panjabi	...	228,954	Tibetan	...	30,023
Pashtu or Afghan	...	20,993	Tulu	...	11,200
Rajmahali	...	6,000			
Sanskrit-Bengali, &c.	...	26,000		Total ...	11,011,605

In addition, the Baptist Bible Translation Society and the American Bible Society have aided the work, especially in Bengali, Assamese, and Oriya.

THE RELIGIOUS TRACT SOCIETY.

At the commencement, Missions were the chief publishers of Christian literature. Valuable aid was rendered in South India by the Christian Knowledge Society, which still co-operates. Some missions, like the Basel Mission and the Methodist Episcopal Church, also publish; but during the last sixty years the Religious Tract Society has been the chief support of Christian literature, exclusive of the Scriptures and Book of Common Prayer. Its grants in 1893 to India, Ceylon and Burma amounted to £3,202.

The first application received by the Religious Tract Society from India for the benefit of the native population was from the Rev. John Gordon of Vizagapatam in 1813. The first Tract Society in India was established by the Rev. John Hands at Bellary in 1817. The Madras Tract Society, the oldest existing Tract Society in India, was established in 1818. The Nagercoil Religious Tract Association was formed in 1822. About 1830 the Neyoor Branch became a separate Society. In 1855 they were united under the title of the South Travancore Tract Society. The dates when other Indian Tract Societies were established are given in the statement below, showing their work during 1893:—

			Subscriptions. Rs.	Sales. Rs.	Nos. Printed. Rs.
1837	Bangalore Tract Society	...	240	15,681†	40,500
1827	Bombay Do.	...	554	32,230†	199,800*
1823	Calcutta Do.	...	2,253	12,629	1,584,077‡
1853	Gujarat Do.	...	318	1,018	58,300
1818	Madras Do.	...	1,413	16,019	1,734,100
1848	North India Do.	...	839	7,380	263,500
1863	Punjab Religious Book Society.		1,310	23,201	209,950
1855	South Travancore Tract Society		380	...	430,000
			6,307	...	4,520,227

† Stationery included.
* Exclusive of 167,200, for the Children's Special Service Mission. ‡ Issues.

The issues of the Indian Tract Societies during the two decades ending in 1891 are given below:—

	1872-81.	1882-91.
Calcutta Tract Society	1,576,251	7,732,265
North India do. ...	660,994	2,727,550
Punjab Religious Book Society ...	339,517	2,215,397
Gujarat Tract Society ...	177,032	623,076
Bombay do.	1,120,404	1,987,810
Madras do.	6,591,891	12,132,652
Bangalore do.	1,580,861	1,915,200
South Travancore do.	1,668,920	1,545,400
	13,715,676	30,879,350

The progress is encouraging.

The Christian Vernacular Education Society, now the Christian Literature Society.

This Society was established in 1858, at the suggestion of the Rev. Henry Venn, as a memorial of the Mutiny. Besides the publication of School books, Mr. Venn hoped that it would relieve the Missions of the training of vernacular teachers and the support of vernacular schools. Two Training Institutions were commenced in Bengal, the Punjab, Western India and South India. The Bengal Institution was soon closed; that at Amritsar was mantained till 1886; the Dindigul Institution till 1889. The Ahmadnagar Institution is still carried on. The missions prefer training their own teachers and having the control of their schools. In Bengal, however, there are about 8,000 children in schools aided by the Society, but under the superintendence of missions. In order to give a better idea of the Society's work, its title was changed in 1890 to the Christian Literature Society. In its publication department considerable prominence has been given to literature in English for educated Hindus.

The statistics for 1893 were briefly as follows:

Children under Instruction	8,215
Students in Training Institution	73
Copies of Publications Printed	1,133,115
Proceeds of Sales	Rs. 72,480

Summary from commencement:

Native Teachers sent into the Mission field...	1,097
Publications printed in 18 languages ...	1,520
Copies printed of do.	19,628,068

THE SALVATION ARMY.

Its work in India was commenced in 1882 by the landing of Commissioner (then Major) Tucker in Bombay, accompanied by 5 other European officers. In 1888 Commissioner Booth Tucker was married to the second daughter of General Booth, and the event was celebrated by the arrival in India of another party of 50 European officers. In 1890 the army had 139 European and 204 native officers, and 1920 native members. The officers, as a rule, are earnest men, but the frequent changes among them have prevented their acquiring a thorough knowledge of the vernaculars, and interfered with their usefulness. Missionaries complain that they go rather to large mission stations than to unoccupied ground.

SUMMARY VIEW OF THE PROGRESS OF CHRISTIANITY IN INDIA.

Moral Revolutions gradual—The opinion has been expressed by Hindus that Christianity will not ultimately prevail in India on account of what they consider its slow progress. It should be remembered that changes do not proceed in the life of a nation as rapidly as in those of an individual, and from its immense population and its caste system, India's advance must be exceptionally gradual. The remarks of an English statesman, Sir J. E. Tennent, who spent several years in Ceylon, deserve consideration :—

"Political changes are usually rapid, and often the offspring of a single cause; but all moral revolutions are of a gradual development, and the result of innumerable agencies. Progressive growth is the law and process of Nature in all her grand operations. Philosophy, science and art, all the moral and intellectual developments of man, are progressive; and under the influence of Christianity itself, the march of civilisation, though controlled and directed by its ascendancy, is regulated by these eternal laws of social progress which have been ordained by omnipotence."

"It is not unreasonable to suppose that the last conquests of Christianity may be achieved with incomparably greater rapidity then has marked its earlier progress and signalised its first success; and that in the instance of India, 'the ploughman may overtake the reaper, the treader of grapes him that soweth the seed, and the type of the prophet realized, that 'a nation shall be born in a day'."*

The progress of Protestant Missions in India since 1851 has been as follows :

	Foreign Missionaries.	Ordained Natives.	Native Christians.	Communicants.	Pupils.
1851 ...	339	21	91,092	14,661	64,043
1861 ...	479	97	138,731	24,976	75,995
1871 ...	488	225	224,258	52,816	122,132
1881 ...	586	461	417,372	113,325	187,652
1890 ...	857	797	559,651	182,722	279,716

* Christianity in Ceylon, pp. 326, 7.

In 1890, divided according to Provinces, they were as follows:

	Foreign Missionaries.	Ordained Natives.	Native Christians.	Communicants.	Pupils.
Bengal ...	186	219	108,901	37,918	50,417
N. W. P. and Oudh.	76	94	30,321	14,722	47,311
Punjab ...	91	50	20,729	6,034	22,523
Central India ...	92	23	11,343	4,580	15,037
Bombay ...	150	48	22,455	9,192	28,120
Madras ...	262	363	365,912	110,276	116,308
Total...	857	797	559,651	182,722	279,716

In 1890 there were 711 European and Eurasian Female Agents, 8,278 Native Christian Female Agents, 71,500 girls in schools, and 32,659 under instruction in Zenanas.

In 1891 the total numbers of Christians—Roman Catholic and Protestant—were as follows:—

Assam ...	16,820
Burma and Andamans ...	121,377
Bengal and Native States ...	191,471
North-West Provinces and Native States ...	58,501
Punjab and Native States ...	57,121
Rajputana ...	4,538
Bombay and Native States ...	170,651
Central Provinces and Native States ...	19,305
Hyderabad and Berar ...	21,788
Mysore ...	38,134
Madras and Native States ...	1,583,466
Total in British India...	2,284,172

Of the above, 1,491,458 are in British Provinces, and 792,714 in Native States. To the above may be added Christians in *French* and *Portuguese* India, amounting to 317,183, making up the total to 2,601,355.

In 1891 Christians ranked fifth in number in British India:—

Hindus ...	207,731,727
Muhammadans ...	57,321,164
Aboriginals ...	9,280,467
Buddhists ...	7,131,361
Christians ...	2,284,172
Sikhs ...	1,907,833
Jains ...	1,416,638
Parsis ...	89,804

It will be seen that in 1891 Christians exceeded the Sikhs by 376,339. In 1881 Christians numbered 1,862,634 and Sikhs 1,853,385, the excess being only 9,249.

But the results of Christianity in India are not to be measured merely by the number of avowed Christians. There are many Christians in heart, who are only prevented from making a public profession by the severe persecution it would entail. In addition, Christianity, in one form or another, is influencing the whole country. Some of the changes produced are noticed below.

I. A CHRISTIAN GOVERNMENT HAS EFFECTED SEVERAL IMPORTANT REFORMS.

The following may be mentioned* :—

1. **The burning or burial alive of widows has been forbidden.**

For thousands of years Hindus considered it a work of great merit to burn their mothers alive with the dead bodies of their husbands. It was the Serampore missionaries who first denounced the custom, though the movement was afterwards taken up by Rammohun Roy. When it was to be abolished by Lord Bentinck, an appeal was made to the Privy Council for its retention. Certain castes buried their widows alive.

2.—**The murder of children has been prohibited.**

Female infants were often destroyed among the Rajputs on account of the foolish expenses incurred at marriages. No punishment followed.

3.—**Human sacrifices have been stopped.**

Mothers sometimes offered their children to the Ganges at Sagar to be devoured by crocodiles. Christian missionaries brought the custom to the notice of Lord Wellesley, who stationed sepoys at Sagar to put a stop to it. Human sacrifices were offered to Kali. The Khonds thought that their lands would not yield crops unless human sacrifices were offered to the earth goddess.

4.—**Suicide has been forbidden.**

Hindus have considered it meritorious to destroy themselves in certain ways. Some drowned themselves at Allahabad; others cast themselves from precipices.

5.—**Barbarous practices have been abolished.**

Criminals are no longer impaled or torn limb by limb by elephants; cutting off the hands of thieves or the noses of women; the extraction of evidence by torture, trial by ordeal, hookswinging, falling on knives, and thigh piercing have been stopped.

6.—**Freedom has been granted to Slaves.**

Human beings can no longer be bought or sold like cattle: cases may still occur, but it is a crime.

7.—**Caste distinctions are not recognized.**

Low castes are allowed to give evidence in courts like any others; high castes are not exempted from appearing.

8.—**The Age of Consent has been raised.**

Brutal mutilation and murders occurred through men having intercourse with their child wives. The age of consent was raised by Lord Lansdowne, although still too low.

9.—**Widow Marriage has been legalized.**

The injustice of Hinduism with regard to widows has thus been strikingly shown by Mr. Justice Ranade :—

---

* Adapted from a list given by Dr. George Smith in his Life of the Rev. Dr. Wilson of Bombay.

"A Hindu widow may not remarry. Against the child-widow the rule prohibiting re-marriage is enforced with inexorable vigour. For them there is no relaxation of this law no pity, no sympathy. But the old Hindu widower, who is shuddering on the verge of the grave, may marry again and again, as often as he likes. For him there is no restriction—he is under no obligation to exercise self-restraint."

It is true that Lord Canning's law has remained nearly a dead letter, but this is the fault of the Hindus.

II.—Social and Moral Reforms have been promoted.

A few illustrations may be given:

1.—**The cruel treatments of widows has excited sympathy.** Mr. Justice Ranade has shown the injustice of Hinduism in forbidding widows to marry. He thus eloquently exposes their wrongs in other respects:

"The child-widow must fast on every *ekadasi* day; if she is a Brahman she must not take even a drop of water. She may die of hunger or thirst, but society has no compassion to show her. She is a *Brahmacharini*. The widower, however, may eat what he likes or how often he likes; he need not fast on the *ekadasi* day; he need not confine himself to one meal a day. He is not a *Brahmachari*. The widow is a *Brahmacharini*. The widower is a man of the world. The widow lives for the benefit of the soul of her deceased lord. Why this distinction between the widower and the widow? Why this hard treatment dealt out to the widow from which the widower is exempt? Under what moral law, under what divine mandate is this inequality of treatment sought to be justified? We know of none, we can think of none. To our mind it is an illustration of the tyranny of the strong ruthlessly exercised over the weak. This huge blot must be wiped out—the curse of God must rest upon a society which from generation to generation observes a custom which involves a huge injustice, and which is degrading to the higher life of humanity."*

2. **Female Education is receiving attention.**—It has been shown that girls' schools for Hindus were first opened by Christian missionaries (see page 37.)

3. **The Brotherhood of Man is beginning to be acknowledged.**—According to Hinduism, England is a land of impure Mlechhas, in which the twice-born should not even temporarily dwell Bathing is necessary to remove the impurity contracted by the touch of its inhabitants. But the cruelty and injustice of Hinduism have been especially shown with regard to the so-called low castes. The treatment accorded to them in the laws of Manu is revolting, and all this is done in the name of religion. Principal Caird well says: "The system of caste involves the worst of all wrongs to humanity—that of hallowing evil by the authority and sanction of religion." The late Dr. Wilson justly characterised caste "as the offspring of pride and deceit, the mainspring of hatred, division, alienation, and tyranny in this great, but alas! still darkened land; the curse of

* Social Science Conference Address.

India for many generations; the unreasonable and fanatical institution which under the grossest misrepresentation and delusion, testified against the full and steady toleration of the British Government."

Juster sentiments are now beginning to be entertained. The words of Burns will yet hold true:

"For a' that, and a' that
Its coming yet, for a' that
That man to man, the world o'er
Shall brothers be for a' that."

4. **The feeling against nautch women.**

Hindus in having dancing girls who are prostitutes are only copying the example set in the heaven of Indra. They are the counterparts of the Apsaras, whose origin the Vishnu Purana and the Ramayana attribute to the churning of the Ocean. The passage in the Ramayana is thus versified by Wilson:

"Then from the agitated deep up sprung
The legion of Apsarases, so named
That to the watery element they owed
Their being. Myriads were they born, and all
In vesture heavenly clad, and heavenly gems;
Yet more divine their native semblance, rich
With all the gifts of grace, of youth and beauty,
A train innumerous followed; yet thus fair,
Nor god nor demon sought their wedded love;
Thus Rághava! they still remain—their charms
The common treasure of the host of heaven."

As stated above, when they came forth from the waters, neither the gods nor the Asuras would have done for wives, so they became common to all. They have the appellations of Surānganās, 'wives of the gods,' and Sumad-ātmajās, 'daughters of pleasure.'*

Two thousand years ago the Greeks had a religion somewhat like that of the Hindus. Their gods fought with each other, and committed adultery. The temple of Venus at Corinth had more than a thousand *hierodouloi*, "servants of the goddess," who were the ruin of many a stranger who visited the city. For several centuries this went on unchecked. Well might it be said by Bishop Lightfoot:

"Imagine, if you can, this licensed shamelessness, this consecrated profligacy, carried on under the sanction of religion and in the full blaze of publicity, while statesmen and patriots, philosophers and men of letters, looked on unconcerned, not uttering one word and not raising one finger to put it down."

The same remark applies to India. For twenty centuries, "statesmen and patriots, philosophers and men of letters" made no attempt to reform such a system. Under Christian influence, a movement has commenced against nautch women. Dancing girls

---

*Dowson's *Dictionary of Hindu Mythology*, p. 19, 20.

in temples are much more objectionable. A feeling against them is beginning to be displayed, as well as against the obscene sculpture on some temples and cars.

5. **Higher Moral Character is beginning to be looked for in public men.**

The feeling awakened at the Tenth National Congress, when an adulterer moved a resolution, is an indication of this, although it also showed that it is still confined to a few. A Resolution was passed by the Social Conference of 1894, that the "private life and morals of public men should be pure and self-denying, as the proper discharge of their duties demands."

6.—**There is a greater regard for Truth.**

Hindu ideas on this point are lax. In the Karna Parva of the Mahabharata, Krishna says: "On an occasion of marriage, or of enjoying a woman, or when life is in danger, or when one's entire property is about to be taken away, or for the sake of a Brahman, falsehood may be uttered. These five kinds of falsehood have been declared sinless." In the Drona Parva he recommended a falsehood to be told. Higher notions are being diffused.

7.—**There is more Honesty and sense of Duty.**

Bribery among officials was formerly almost general. Though it still prevails to some extent among the lower orders, there is a great improvement.

III. Hindu Religious Ideas are being Christianised.

1.—**Higher conceptions of God are being entertained.**

There is an Indian proverb, *Yatah devah, tatha bhaktah*, "As is the god, so is the worshipper." The conception which a person has of God, exerts a powerful influence upon his character.

Hindus have two ideas of God—the *nirguna* Brahma and gods like Vishnu or Siva. The first is supposed to exist in a state of dreamless repose; the others have the characteristics of Hindu rajas, although with vastly increased powers.

Hindu books contain some sublime descriptions of the natural attributes of God, but these qualities are often understood in an imperfect sense. Though God is represented as *sarvasakta*, almighty, yet He cannot *create* anything, that is, call it into existence out of nothing. God is often called *dayalur*, merciful. Mercy is doing good to one who does not merit it; but according to Hinduism God cannot do anything irrespective of the good and evil deeds of the soul. In the Rig Veda Book viii. Hymn 85, Indra is called the "holiest of the holy," yet he is represented as notorious for drunkenness, and in the Mahabharata he is described as the "adulterous lover of Ahalya." Monotheism is now beginning to be acknowledged; Vishnu and Siva are allowed to have no existence, but to be the inventions of men who framed gods after their own evil hearts. God is acknowledged to be a holy Being, and instead of being regardless of His creatures, is supposed to listen to their petitions.

2.—**Religion and Morality are not divorced.**—A very immoral man may be a devout Hindu. The story of Ajamila is well known. He said to have been all his life guilty of the worst crimes; but because, in the hour of death, he said, "Narayana, Narayana, Narayana, give me some water;" Vishnu took him to heaven. Sounder views on this point are making progress.

3.—**More correct ideas of Religious Worship are being entertained**:—Hindu worship on festival nights consists merely in drumming and shouting, in flags, and guns and fire-works, in the dragging of the idol car by tumultuous noisy crowds, in singing and dancing, in all sorts of shows, noises, and riots. When this worship is being performed, no instruction is ever given in the duties of life. The discharge of these duties is never represented as enjoined by the gods. No prayers are offered by the worshippers to enable them to discharge these duties aright. Contrast with this religious worship among the Bramhos, adopted from Christianity. It is beginning to be acknowledged that bathing in certain rivers or drinking the filthy water of certain tanks, cannot wash away sin.

In all the above ways, the influence of Christianity has been felt in India by millions who have not embraced it.

THE PROSPECTS OF CHRISTIANITY IN INDIA.

There is a well-known saying that "History repeats itself." From the history of the past we can form some idea of the future. Under like circumstances, like events will probably happen. The point to be established is that the situation of India is now analogous to that of ancient Europe, and the changes which took place there will be repeated in India.

The parallel between Ancient Europe and Modern India may be shown as follows:

I.—In Religion they resemble one another.

The old Aryans once lived together, worshipping the same gods. The Eastern Aryans, after coming to India, gradually gave up the Vedic gods, and adopted those of the Puranas. Eighteen centuries ago the religion of ancient Europe very much resembled that of modern India. Gods and goddesses were numbered by thousands. A short account may be given of Jupiter and his wife Juno.

JUPITER.

JUNO.

Jupiter was considered the most powerful of the gods. His father Saturn had received the kingdom of the world on condition of not raising up male children. He therefore devoured them as soon as they were born. His wife, Ops, when Jupiter was born, secreted him, and gave Saturn a stone which he swallowed under the supposition that it was a male child! When only a year old, Jupiter was strong enough to conquer the Titans, or Asurs, who had imprisoned his father. Saturn afterwards conspired against his son's life, and was banished. Jupiter divided the empire of the world between himself and his brothers. He reserved heaven to himself, gave the sea to Neptune, and the lower regions to Pluto. He married Juno and several other wives. To gratify his lust he assumed various forms. In the Puranas similar stories are related of some of the Hindu gods. Juno, called the queen of the heaven, was said to be the sister and wife of Jupiter. She frequently upbraided her husband for his adulteries, as Parvati is said to have reproved Siva.

One of Jupiter's concubines was a very clever goddess, named Metis. Afraid lest her child should be wiser than himself, Jupiter devoured her when pregnant. Some time after, feeling a great pain in the head, he ordered Vulcan to cleave it open. The goddess Minerva then sprang forth, fully armed! As Minerva was born from Jupiter's head, Juno wished to have a son of her own without her husband. She is said to have brought forth Vulca by only smelling a certain plant. The Hindus have a similar able that Parvati formed Ganesa from the scurf of her body.

The supposed gods of the Greeks and Romans behaved vell much like those of the Hindus. They quarrelled and fought with each other, and were guilty of all kinds of crime. Men excuse their evil deeds by the example of Jupiter. "How could a morta have greater power than a god?"

The cities were full of temples and priests; there were ceremonies and processions like those in India. Idols were so numerous in Athens, that it was said to be easier to find a god than a man. Nearly every city had its local deity, to whom it looked for protection, and whose supremacy it acknowledged.

II.—Politically, Ancient Europe and Modern India resemble each other.

Ancient Europe.—Eighteen centuries ago, the Mediterranean was a Roman lake. All the countries around it were under one government. Formerly they were often at war with one another, hindering intercourse. The *Pax Romana* (Roman peace) "broke down the boundaries of rival races, and levelled barriers to the spread of Christianity." By enabling all to travel freely, local prejudices were softened, and a cosmopolitan feeling was awakened which was some preparation for the universal spiritual feeling which was sought to be established. Travelling was facilitated by a net-work of roads extending from Rome to every part of the empire. Merchant ships covered the Mediterranean. An Alexandrian ship, bound to Rome with corn, afforded a passage to the Apostle Paul.

In ancient Europe a knowledge of the Greek language was very widely diffused. The New Testament was written in Greek, and wherever Christian missionaries travelled, they were able to make themselves understood in that language.

Roman law and justice, for some time, granted religious toleration, although afterwards, when political fears were aroused by the spread of Christianity, the whole power of the State was exerted in vain to crush it.

Modern India.—It is remarkable in how many respects India now resembles Europe when the Gospel was first brought to its shores. Formerly India was divided into numerous states, frequently at war with one another, preventing free communication. The *Pax Britannica* enables all to travel without hindrance from the Himalayas to Cape Comorin. Roads, railways, and steam-vessels afford facilities for moving about never possessed before. Through them it has been found practicable to hold a National Congress. Max Müller says, "The Indian never knew the feeling of nationality." The Hindus love their children, they are zealous for their caste; but formerly their sympathies did not extend beyond these narrow limits. Enlightened Hindus now look more at their country as a whole. The English language is tending powerfully to weld together educated men of different nationalities, to break down prejudices. India is the seat of caste, which splits up its races into small sections, regarding each other with mutual jealousy. Ideas of the "brotherhood of man" are gradually being diffused.

Hinduism is at once most tolerant and intolerant. It will allow a man to believe anything or nothing, but woe to him if he breaks the laws of caste. Until the *Lex Loci* Act of the British Government was passed, a Hindu becoming a Christian was stript of his property. A Hindu, on his baptism, has been driven out of his home by his parents with the curse of their gods. British law has, as far as it can, secured religious toleration in India. It seeks to carry out the Proclamation, "that none be in any wise favoured, none molested or disquieted by reason of their religious faith or observances; but that *all* shall alike enjoy the equal and impartial protection of the law."

III.—The Change which took place in Europe.

When Christian missionaries first came to Europe, they were often treated with contempt. Of the Apostle Paul at Athens, it was asked by the philosophers, "What will this babbler say?" When Christianity began to make progress, two methods were adopted to check it—persecution and attempts to purify the popular religion.

Christians suffered from severe persecution on the following accounts:

It was formerly thought that a king had a right to compel his subjects to worship his god. If they refused, they were regarded as disloyal. The one universal religion throughout the Roman empire was the worship of the emperor as a god. The people generally were quite willing to add one more deity to the number they already worshipped. But it was different with the Christians. "To prove your obedience to the emperor," said a Roman governor to Achatius, "sacrifice with us to his honour." Upon this Achatius explained. "I pray to God for my emperor, but a sacrifice neither should he require nor we pay. Who may offer divine honours to a man?" Upon this declaration he was sentenced to death.

Some disliked Christianity because it interfered with their gains. There were many persons engaged in image-making, in providing sacrifices, and as priests in the temples. With the spread of Christianity, the demand for idols decreased, and there were fewer offerings at the shrines.

It was thought that the prosperity of a country depended upon the worship of its gods. Christians had no images and did not offer sacrifices; so they were regarded as atheists, men without any religion. Earthquakes, famine and pestilence were looked upon as calamities sent by the offended deities for the neglect of their worship. The execution of the Christians was supposed to be the best means of propitiating them. The cry was immediately raised, "The Christians to the lions!" The same idea prevails, more or less, in India. In Tinnevelly numbers have become Christians.

If there is an outbreak of cholera, it is attributed to the anger of the demons at no longer being worshipped.

The most horrible reports were spread about the Christians. They were said at their meetings to be guilty of the practices of the Vamacharis in India, as well as to kill and eat little children. Even the best of the Romans regarded Christianity as a "hateful superstition," and its followers were styled "enemies of the human race." When Paul first came to Rome, the Jews told him that "everywhere this sect is spoken against."

The attempts to check the progress of Christianity by persecution failed. There was even a proverb, "The blood of the martyrs is the seed of the Church." The more Christians were persecuted, the more they increased, and at last idolatry disappeared in the Roman empire.

Another method adopted to check Christianity was to purify the popular religion, and to copy some of the features of Christianity. The immoral stories about Jupiter and other gods were treated as allegories, and spiritual meanings were given to disgraceful rites. Christians had been scoffed at on account of "their practice of instructing artisans and old women in religious matters." Now the heathen priests were urged to teach the people; like the Christians, they were to care for the poor. Christian conceptions regarding sin and salvation were adopted to some extent. The heathen now believed that they possessed the excellencies which Christianity was conceded to contain, without its defects.

All these efforts proved vain. After a struggle of about three centuries Christianity triumphed, and the Roman Emperor avowed himself a Christian.

The Effects of Christianity in Ancient Europe.—These are thus described by Gladstone:

"Christianity both produced a type of character wholly new to the Roman world, and it fundamentally altered the laws and institutions, the tone, temper, and traditions of that world. For example, it changed profoundly the relation of the poor to the rich, and the almost forgotten obligations of the rich to the poor. It abolished slavery, it abolished human sacrifices, abolished gladiatorial shows, and a multitude of other horrors. It restored the position of women in society. It proscribed polygamy, and put down divorce, absolutely in the West, though not absolutely in the East. It made peace, instead of war, the normal and presumed relation between human societies. It exhibited life as a discipline everywhere, and in all its parts, and changed essentially the place and function of suffering in human experience. Accepting the ancient morality as far as it went, it not only enlarged, but transfigured its teaching by the laws of humility and of forgiveness, and by a law of purity perhaps even more new and strange than these:......

"All this was not the work of a day, but it was the work of powers and principles which persistently asserted themselves in despite of controversy, of infirmity, and of corruption in every form; which reconstituted in life and vigour a society formed in decadence; which by degrees came to pervade the very air we breathe; and which eventually have beyond all dispute made Christendom the dominant portion, and Christianity the ruling power of the world."*

IV.—The Change which will take place in India.

In India, Christians are not persecuted by Government as in ancient Europe, but Hinduism does so as far it can. It will indeed, tolerate any religious opinions that do not interfere with its caste laws. It has, therefore, well been urged that Hinduism is, strictly speaking, not a religion, but a social organization. Religion is defined to be, "the performance of our duties of love and obedience towards God." A Hindu may ignore these entirely. Guru Prosad Sen says:

> "A Hindu may choose to have a faith and creed, if he wants a creed, or to do without one. He may be an atheist, a deist, a monotheist, or a polytheist, a believer in the Vedas or Shastras, or a sceptic as regards their authority, and his position as a Hindu cannot be questioned by anybody because of his belief or unbelief, so long as he conforms to social rules."†

As attempts were made in ancient Europe to purify heathenism, so similar efforts are being made by some in India to frame a New Hinduism, which will bear the fierce light of the nineteenth century. The leading Bengali novelist tried to whitewash Krishna; spiritual meanings have been given to his adulteries. Doctrines, essentially Christian, have been claimed to be Hindu. Christian worship has been adopted to some extent. In Madras a *Hindu* Young Men's Association has been formed in imitation of *Christian* Associations. Some years ago Sir Madhava Row advocated the "judicious *revival* or *repair* of Hinduism." Some are so satisfied with their reforms that they think they have devised a system superior to Christianity. But such attempts will share the same fate they did in ancient Europe.

A National Religion.—A desire is expressed by some educated Hindus for a *National* religion. It is thought degrading to India to have any other religion than her own.

There is no national geography, astronomy, chemistry, geometry, &c. Science is one all the world over. It is the same with religion. If each country had its own God, there might be different religions; but all enlightened men are now agreed that there is

---

* *Nineteenth Century*, May, 1888, pp. 783, 784.

† *Introduction to the Study of Hinduism*, pp. 2, 3.

only one God, the Creator, Preserver, and Governor of the Universe. The Brotherhood of Man is similarly acknowledged:

> "Children, we are all
> Of one great Father, in whatever clime,
> His providence hath cast the seed of life:
> All tongues, all colours."

Since God is one and all men are alike His children, it is reasonable to suppose that He has given only one religion. A *national* religion shows that it is not the *true* religion.

The most enlightened countries in Europe and America accepted a religion first made known to them by Asiatics, and did not reject it from false patriotism, saying, "We must have national religions."

An Indian poet says: "Disease born with you will destroy you: the medicine which is in the lofty mountain not born with you, will expel the disorder."

Of all false patriotism that is the worst which seeks by sophistry to defend erroneous beliefs because they are national. It promotes hypocrisy and disregard of truth among its advocates, while it is a grievous wrong to their ignorant countrymen, tending to perpetuate the reign of superstition.

Let the advocates of a national religion remember the wise words of Sir Madhava Row:—

"What is not true is not patriotic."

The Future Religion of India.—A distinguished French Orientalist says that as India has already adopted the science and arts of Christian nations, so she will one day spontaneously embrace their faith.

India has adopted the science of Christian nations. No educated Hindu now believes in Mount Meru, in seas of ghi, wine, &c., or that eclipses are caused by Asurs seeking to seize the sun and moon. The arts of Christian nations have also been accepted. Railways, the use of the electric telegraph, photographs, weaving by steam power, &c., have been introduced, and are freely employed. The Indian would be looked upon as an idiot who urged his countrymen to stick to the "national" conveyances of palanquins and bullock carts, and not travel by the "foreign" invention of railways.

It has already been shown how Christianity is influencing and elevating Indian public opinion. For many centuries some Hindu temples had the most indecent sculptures, prostitutes took a prominent part in their religious services, without a voice being raised against them. The Penal Code punished people who sell or expose obscene books, pictures, or statues; but permits such things in the name of religion. Some educated Hindus, through the spread of Christian light, are beginning to protest against such abominations. A woman, according to Hinduism, is denied religious instruction, and taught that she has simply to consider her husband as her God. Under Christian influence, female education is spreading, and the just rights of women, long denied, are beginning to be acknowledged, though not yet conceded.

The Brotherhood of Man, diametrically opposed to the caste system, is gradually commending itself, for its truth, justice and tendency to promote the general happiness. There is now a greater desire than ever before to seek the common good, instead of selfishly consulting one's own ease and comfort.

Already Indian Christians number above two millions, and they are increasing every year. One of the most eloquent speakers at the National Congresses is a Bengali Christian.

The Bible says, "The gods that have not made the heavens and the earth, even they shall perish from the earth and from under these heavens." It also contains many prophecies regarding the spread of Christianity. It was foretold of Jesus Christ, "His name shall endure for ever; men shall be blessed in Him, and all nations shall call Him blessed;" "His dominion is an everlasting dominion which shall not pass away;" "The isles shall wait for His law, and in His name shall the nations trust." These prophecies we see being fulfilled before our eyes.

The change of religion which took place in Europe, in spite of the strongest opposition of the Roman Government, will also happen in India. The temples of Vishnu and Siva will yet be as deserted as those of Jupiter and Minerva in Europe. The Eastern and Western Aryans will kneel at the same footstool, and offer the same grand old prayer, beginning, "Our Father which art in heaven." When this change will take place, we do not know. It took three centuries to overthrow heathenism in ancient Europe, and it may take as long in modern India. Light, however, is spreading, and an Indian Luther may yet arise to bring about a rapid reformation.

HOW INDIA WOULD BE BENEFITED BY THE ADOPTION OF CHRISTIANITY.

Only a brief summary can be given under this head.

THE POLITICAL ADVANTAGES.

These are strikingly shown by Mr. B. L. CHANDRA, of Calcutta, in a letter to the Delegates to the National Congress. Space permits only a few quotations.

"The chief aim of what has been termed the 'NATIONAL MOVEMENT' out of which 'the Congress movement sprung,' was 'The fusion into one national whole of all the different, and till recently, discordant elements that constitute the population of India." (Mr. Hume's *Allahabad Speech,* April 30, 1888).

What now stands in the way of our obtaining those privileges which the Congress asks from Government? Is it not the fact that the peoples of India do not represent a united Nation, but are made up of numberless different and discordant races and nationalities? Lord Dufferin said in Calcutta: 'In the present condition of India there can be no real or effectual representation of the people, with their enormous numbers, their multifarious interests, and their tesselated nationalities.'

"The problem is, how can the several distinct nationalities which constitute the population of India, with their infinitely diverse rites, discordent and hostile prejudices, and conflicting social usages, be fused into one Nation?"

A great authority has said that, 'Religion is the strongest and most important of all the elements which go to constitute nationality.

But is there a religion, it may be fairly asked, which can weld the various peoples and races of India, into one united nation? What is the religion that can knit the Hindoo and the Moslem, the Aryan and the Aboriginal, in the bonds of one great Brotherhood? What is the religion that can harmonize into one nationality the Sikhs and the Parsees, the Rohillas and the Pathans, the Biluchees and the Assamese? What, in a word, is the religion that can make the Brahmin and the Chandal one? How shall this vision of unity become an historical reality?

Hinduism cannot achieve this unity. With its inexorable caste rules, it can separate and divide, but can never unite and harmonize. Some people think that the Government, with its official representatives, is the greatest enemy of the Congress. If these would consider the matter without prejudice, they would say that the greatest enemy of the Congress and the country, are the HINDOO REVIVALISTS. The revival of Hindooism means wider separation, further disunion, deeper antagonism between race and race; it means rending asunder, not union. Educated Indians, therefore, who truly love their country and long for the 'fusion into one national whole of all the different elements that constitute the population of India,' should beware of Hindoo revivalists.

But that which from its very nature Hindooism is unfitted to do, it is one of the chief missions of Christianity to accomplish. Christianity came to proclaim to the world the Fatherhood of God and the Brotherhood of Man in a sense in which they never were proclaimed before. Christianity knows no caste. It knows no distinction of race or country.

"Since the Roman society and polity began to decay, men enthusiastically imbued with the spirit of Christianity, have ever been foremost in the task of building up that fabric of European

Civilization which now dominates over the world. Whether in the wilds of Scandinavia or among idolatrous Teuton hordes, in the cloister, in the camp, in the parliament, or in the guild of mediæval Europe—or, in later ages, asserting by speech, by pen, or by the sword, the rights and obligations of mankind—the strongest and most successful organizers and constructors, social as well as political, have ever been men of the strongest, deepest, most earnest religious Christian convictions, all deriving their inspiration from one common source."

Gentlemen of the Congress! What Christianity has done for the most powerful nations of Europe, what it has done for the United States of America, it can and will do for India. Political rights, large powers of administration, the representative and constitutional form of Government, equality, fraternity, unity, all these things, the very privileges which we seek for, have followed as a matter of course, wherever Christianity has been accepted and loyally followed. Christianity therefore has a peculiar claim upon your attention.*

Material and Social Advantages.

Christianity has no restrictions against foreign travel. England has been enriched partly by its foreign commerce. Manual labour is considered honourable, and manufactures are thus encouraged. India is called the "Land of Charity," but it is also the "Land of Beggars," from the false charity promoted by Hinduism. Money would no longer be worse than uselessly spent on Shraddhas.

Caste has been justly called the "most inexorable social tyranny ever inflicted on the human race." Its restrictions would be swept away. The *stomach* has been called the seat of Hinduism, Christianity teaches that a man is defiled, not by what he eats, but by evil thoughts, evil words, and evil deeds. A Christian is not afraid lest people should see him eat, lest his food should be polluted by the shadow of any person; he can take pure water from any hand. Christianity has no restriction about marriage except between near relations. It is well known what troubles fall upon the Hindus in this respect in consequence of their absurd caste rules.

Moral and Religious Advantages.

Obscene images would no longer deface temples; dancing girls would not take part in religious worship; idols, giving debasing ideas of God, would be swept away. It has been shown that men are powerfully influenced by the character of their deities.

* See the whole paper. Sold by Mr. A. T. Scott, Tract Depot, Madras. Price ½ Anna.

If a man worships a god said to be guilty of lying, theft, adultery, and murder, the effect must be evil. On the other hand, the adoration of a Being infinite on justice, purity, and love, must have an elevating influence.

For their salvation in another world, Hindus trust to refuges of lies, which will fail them in the day of trial. They are taught to believe that their sins can be washed away by bathing in certain rivers or tanks, by pilgrimages to certain places.

All these are delusions. There are no such beings as Vishnu, Siva, or Durga. Hinduism is an invention of priestcraft to enrich Brahmans.

Christianity leads us from the FALSE TO THE TRUE—from imaginary deities, stained with vice, to the one living and true God of spotless purity and boundless benevolence. Its two great commands are LOVE TO GOD and LOVE TO MAN. It acknowledges our sinful condition, our helplessness, but it provides an Almighty Saviour, suited to our needs, and the influences of the Holy Spirit to cleanse our souls.

Let the reader not be content to float, like a dead fish, with the current of Hindu Society, caring only for his ease and the favour of the ignorant and superstitious. Let him accept himself the Gospel of Christianity, and seek to have a part in the glorious enterprise of elevating, in every respect, the many millions of this great country, the land of his birth.

INDEX.

	Page.
Abdul Masih, Rev.	57
Afghans	73
Alexandria	3
A. L. O. E.	67
Am. Meth. Episcopal Mission ...	61
Anderson, Rev. John	104
Arya Samaj	66
Assamese	40
Badagas	112
Badley, Rev. Dr. B. H.... ...	62
Baker, Rev. H. ...	115
Basel Mission... ...	109; 116
Bengalis	21
Beschi, Father	10
Bhils...	84
Bible Societies	120
Do. Translations	117
Bowley, Rev. W.	58
Brahma Samaj	37
Braidwood, Rev. J.	104
Brown, Rev. David	29
Buchanan, Rev. Dr. C.... ...	27
Butler, Rev. Dr. W.	61
Caldwell, Bishop	96
Cambridge University Mission...	61
Canarese	107
Carey, Rev. W.	25
Chamberlain, Rev. J.	58
Chota Nagpore	51
Christian Literature Society ...	123
Christianity in India, Progress...	123
Do. Prospects..	123
Do. Statistics..	123
Clark, Rev. R.	67
Clough, Rev. J. E.	90
Corrie, Bishop D.	59
Day, Rev. S. S.	89
Duff, Rev. Dr.	34
Duthie, Rev. J.	99
Europe, Ancient	128
Female Education	36

	Page.
Forman, Rev. Dr. W. C. ...	67
French, Bishop T. V.	68
Garos	46
Glasgow, Rev. James	77
Gonds	85
Gossner's Mission	53
Government Reforms	125
Gujaratis	76
Hands, Rev. John	108
Hay, Rev. Dr. John	89
Heber, Bishop	30
Hindi	55
Hindustani	54
Hippalus	2
Hodson, Rev. T.	109
Imad-ud-din, Rev. Dr.... ...	69
Jagannath, Temple	47
Jewett, Rev. L.	89
Keshab Chunder Sen	39
Khasis	43
Kiernander, J. Z.	24
Kois	86
Kols...	51
Lepchas	45
Leupolt, Rev. C. B.	59
Lynch, Rev. J.	102
Madura Mission	103
Marathi Missions	76
Malayalis	113
Marshman, Joshua	26
Martyn, Henry	56
Mateer, Rev. S.	4
Menezes, Archbishop	5
Middleton, Bishop	29
Mikirs	43
Miller, Rev. Dr. W.	105
Mitchell, Rev. Dr. M.	81
Moral Reforms	126
Mullens, Rev. Dr. J.	33
Mundaris	51

	Page.
Nagas	41
National Religion, A	134
Nautch Women	127
Nehemiah Goreh, Rev.	59
Newton, Rev. Dr. John	66
Nilgiri Tribes	111
Noble, Rev. R.	91
Oraons	51
Oriyas	46
Oxford Mission	36
Pandita Ramabai	84
Panjabis	64
Pantænus	3
Pathans	73
Pfander, Rev. Dr.	74
Plutschau, Henry	11
Rajagopaul, Rev. P.	104
Rajputana Mission	63
Rammohun Roy	37
Religious Tract Society	121
Rice, Rev. B.	109
Ringletaube, Rev. W. T.	98
Robert de Nobili	10
Roman Catholic Missions	8
Salvation Army	123
Sanskrit Bible	117
Santals	48
Sargent, Bishop	100
Satthianadhan, Rev. W. T.	100
Schultze, Rev. B.	96
Schwartz, C. F.	15
Scudder, Rev. H. M.	107
Sherring, Rev. M. A.	2, 60
Shoolbred, Rev. Dr. W.	64
Sikhs	64
Sindis	75
Smith, Dr. G.	2
Social Reform	126
Statistics of Indian Missions	123
Syrian Christians	3
Tamils	94
Telugus	87
Thoburn, Bishop	62
Thomas, St.	2
Tibetans	69
Todas	111
Travancore	114
Tulus	113
Ullmann, Rev. J. F.	61
Urdu	55
Ward, William	26
Weitbrecht, Rev. J. J.	33
Wenger, Rev. Dr.	31
Wilson, Rev. Dr. John	81
Xavier, Francis	9
Yates, Rev. Dr.	31
Zenana Missions	37, 116
Ziegenbalg, B.	11

ENGLISH PUBLICATIONS FOR INDIAN READERS.

Papers on Indian Reform.

This is a Series of Papers treating of the great questions connected with Indian progress—material and moral.

SOCIAL REFORM.

ON DECISION OF CHARACTER AND MORAL COURAGE. 8vo. 56 pp. 1½ As. Post-free, 2 As.

A reprint of Foster's celebrated Essay, with some remarks on its application to India.

SANITARY REFORM IN INDIA. 55 pp. 2 As. Post-free, 2½ As.

How lakhs of Lives may be saved every year, aud crores of cases of Sickness prevented; Precautions against Fever, Cholera, Diabetes, &c.

IS INDIA BECOMING POORER OR RICHER? WITH REMEDIES FOR THE EXISTING POVERTY. 8vo. 82 pp. 2½ As. Post-free, 3 As.

The prevailing idea with regard to the increasing poverty of India shown to be incorrect, and the true means of promoting its wealth explained.

DEBT AND THE RIGHT USE OF MONEY. 8vo. 32 pp. 1 Anna.

Prevalence of Debt in India; its Causes; Evils; how to get out of it; with Franklin's Way to Wealth, &c.

PURITY REFORM. 8vo. 32 pp. 1 Anna.

The great need of this reform shown, and the means for its promotion.

CASTE. 8vo. 66 pp. 2 As. Post-free, 2½ As.

Supposed and real origin of Caste; Laws of Caste according to Manu; its Effects; Duty with regard to it.

THE WOMEN OF INDIA AND WHAT CAN BE DONE FOR THEM. 8vo 158 pp. 4 As. Post-free, 5½ As.

Women in Hindu literature; Female Education; Marriage Customs; Widow Marriage; means to be adopted to raise the Position of Women.

THE ABOVE COMPLETE IN ONE VOLUME, 1 Rupee Net. Postage, 2½ As.

RELIGIOUS REFORM.

POPULAR HINDUISM. 8vo. 96 pp. 2½ As. Post-free, 3½ As.

Review of the Hinduism of the Epic Poems and Puranas, &c.; Rites and Observances; Effects of Hinduism, and Suggested Reforms.

PHILOSOPHIC HINDUISM. 8vo. 72 pp. 2½ Annas. Post-free, 3 As.

The Upanishads; the Six Schools of Hindu Philosophy; the Minor Schools; Doctrines of Philosophic Hinduism; the Bhagavad Gita; Causes of the Failure of Hindu Philosophy; &c.

AN ACCOUNT OF THE VEDAS, WITH ILLUSTRATIVE EXTRACTS. 8vo. 166 pp. 4½ Annas. Post-free, 6 Annas.

The principal Divisions of Vedas are described; with life in Vedic times, the gods of the Vedas, the offerings and sacrifices. Some of the most important hymns from the ten Mandalas are quoted in full. Extracts are also given from the Atharva Veda and the Brahmanas.

THE BRAHMA SAMAJ, AND OTHER MODERN ECLECTIC RELIGIOUS SYSTEMS, 108 pp. 3 As. Post-free, 4 Annas.

Modern Hindu Theism; Rammohun Roy; Debendranath Tagore; Keshub Chunder Sen; the Sadharan Brahmo Samaj; Madras Brahmoism; Prarthana Samajes; Brahmist Doctrines and Prospects. With Portraits of Rammohun Roy, Debendranath Tagore, and Keshub Chunder Sen.

INDIA HINDU, AND INDIA CHRISTIAN; OR, WHAT HINDUISM HAS DONE FOR INDIA, AND WHAT CHRISTIANITY WOULD DO FOR IT. 8vo. 72 pp. 2½ Annas. Post-free, 3 Annas.

Address to thoughtful Hindus, showing how much their country would benefit from the religion which many of them now oppose.

THE ABOVE COMPLETE IN ONE VOLUME, 1 Rupee Net. Postage, 2½ As.

CHRISTIANITY EXPLAINED TO A HINDU: OR, THE DOCTRINES OF CHRISTIANITY AND HINDUISM COMPARED. 60 pp. 2 As.

Doctrines about God, Creation, and Soul, Karma, Transmigration, Sin, Incarnations, Salvation, Prospects at Death, and Comparative Effects.

TESTIMONIES OF GREAT MEN TO THE BIBLE AND CHRISTIANITY. 8vo. 45 pp. 1½ As. Post-free, 2 As.

Opinions expressed by great writers, philosophers, scientists, lawyers and statesmen, showing that the Bible and Christianity are firmly believed by the most eminent men of the time.

HOW THE PEOPLE OF ANCIENT EUROPE BECAME CHRISTIANS, AND THE FUTURE RELIGION OF INDIA. 8vo. 48 pp. 1½ As. Post-free, 2 As.

An account of the Eastern and Western Aryans; their common origin; resemblance in language and religion; how Christianity was first brought to Europe; the opposition it encountered, and its final success; with the evidence that it will follow a similar course in India.

THE GREAT TEMPLES OF INDIA, CEYLON AND BURMA. Imperial 8vo. 104 pp. with 60 illustrations. 6 As. Post-free, 7½ As.

There are pictures and descriptions of some of the most celebrated Hindu, Sikh, Jain, and Buddhist temples; as Puri, Budh-Gaya, Benares, Hurdwar, Gangotri, Ellora, Elephanta, Amritsar, Gwalior, Tanjore, Srirangam, Kandy, Prome and Mandalay.

KRISHNA, AS DESCRIBED IN THE PURANAS AND BHAGAVAD GITA. 8vo. 71 pp. 2½ As. Post-free, 3 As.

A full account is given of the Krishna Avatara, chiefly taken from the Vishnu Purana, with some extracts from the Bhagavata Purana and the Mahabharata; the circumstances which led to the great war between the Pandus and Kurus are described; and some of the doctrines of the Bhagavad Gita are examined in detail.

ACCOUNT OF THE TEMPLE OF JAGANNATH AT PURI. 8vo. 48 pp. 1½ As. Post-free, 2 As.

The account is taken chiefly from Dr. Rajendralala Mitra's *Antiquities of Orissa*; Hunter's *Gazetteer of India*, Sterling's *Orissa*, &c. With views of the temple, procession, and images.

CIVILIZATION, ANCIENT AND MODERN, COMPARED; WITH REMARKS ON THE STUDY OF SANSKRIT. 8vo. 48 pp. 1½ As. Post-free, 2 As.

Hindu Civilization in the Vedic and Puranic Periods, contrasted with that of modern times. The accounts of the former have been largely taken from Mr. R. C. Dutt's *Civilization in Ancient India.*

TRACTS FOR MUHAMMADANS. 12mo. 120 pp. 3 As.

By the Rev. Dr. G. H. Rouse, M. A. Translated from the Bengali. The Integrity of the Gospel; Jesus or Muhammad?; The Sinless Prophet; The True Islam; The Koran; Fatiha; The Paraclete, &c. are some of the subjects.

Pice Papers on Indian Reform, ¼ Anna Each.

Some are original; others are abridged from the foregoing for popular use.

1. Love of Hoarding and Jewelry.
2. Marriage and Shraddha Expenses.
3. Supposed and Real Causes of Disease.
4. Patriotism: False and True.
5. Management of Infants.
6. Debt, and How to Get Out of it.
7. The Purdah: or, the Seclusion of Indian Women.
8. Caste: its Origin and Effects.
9. Astrology.
10. What has the British Government done for India?
11. Who wrote the Vedas?
12. Manava-Dharma Sastra.
13. The Bhagavad Gita.
14. The Science of the Hindu Sastras.
15. Fevers: their Causes, Treatment, and Prevention.
16. Cholera and Bowel Complaints.
17. Animal Worship.
18. Early Marriage, its Evils and Suggested Reforms.
19. Duty to a Wife.
20. The Fruits of Hinduism.

The above complete in one volume, 10 Annas.

21. Indian Widows and what should be done for them.
22. The Advantages of Female Education.
23. Hindu and Christian Worship Compared.
24. Hindu Pilgrimages.
25. Charity: False and True.
26. The Two Watchwords—Custom and Progress.
27. The Value of Pure Water.
28. Charms, Mantras and other Superstitions.
29. Nautches.
30. Importance of Cleanliness.
31. How to have Healthy Children.
32. How to bring up Children.
33. How to take Care of the Sick.
34. Eclipses.
35. Family Prayer.
36. Giving abuse.

Exposures of Theosophy.

The Theosophic Craze: its History; the Great Mahatma Hoax; How Mrs. Besant was Befooled and Deposed; its attempted Revival of Exploded Superstitions of the Middle Ages. 8vo. 96 pp. 3 As. Post-free, 4 As.

INDIA, PAST AND PRESENT. 8vo. 96 pp. 2 Annas. Post-free, 2½ As.

It is considered whether India would benefit more from Hindu or Western Civilization, from Sanskrit or English; with a notice of India's Present Needs. Theosophist plans for the improvement of India are examined.

Papers for Thoughtful Hindus.

No. 1. THE RELATION OF CHRISTIANITY AND HINDUISM. 8vo. 32 pp. By the Rev. Dr. KRISHNA MOHUN BANERJEA, late Sanskrit Examiner to the Calcutta University. ½ An.

The remarkable resemblances, in some respects, between ancient Hinduism and Christianity are pointed out.

No. 2. THE SUPPOSED AND REAL DOCTRINES OF HINDUISM, AS HELD BY EDUCATED HINDUS. 8vo. 32 pp. By the REV. NEHEMIAH (NILAKANTH) GOREH. ½ Anna.

It is shown that the belief of educated Hindus with regard to God, His Attributes, Creation, &c., are not found in the Vedas; but have been derived from Christianity.

No. 3. MORAL COURAGE. 8vo. 32 pp. ½ Anna.

A lecture by the Bishop of Bombay.

No. 4. THE IMPORTANCE OF RELIGION. 8vo. 48 pp. ¾ Anna.

An appeal to the young, by John Foster, author of Essay on *Decision of Character*.

No. 5. CHRISTIANITY, OR—WHAT? 8vo. 16 pp. ½ An. By the Rev. H. Rice.

Christianity is shown to be the only religion which meets the wants of man.

No. 6. THE SENSE OF SIN IN THE LIGHT OF HISTORY. A lecture by the Rev. F. W. KELLETT, M. A., Madras Christian College. 8vo. 20 pp. Price ½ Anna.

It is shown that the deeper the sense of sin, the more mature the religious life.

No. 7. BISHOP CALDWELL ON KRISHNA AND THE BHAGAVAD GITA. 8vo. 32 pp. ¾ An.

A Reprint of "Remarks on the late Hon. Sadagopah Charloo's Introduction to a Report of a Pamphlet, entitled 'Theosophy of the Hindus,'" with a Preface by the Rev. J. L. Wyatt.

No. 8. THE DUTIES OF EDUCATED YOUNG MEN OF INDIA 8vo. 16 pp. ½ Anna.

By the Rev. H. Ballantine.

Descriptions of Countries and Peoples.

PICTORIAL TOUR ROUND INDIA. Imperial 8vo. 116 pp. 6 As. Post-free, 7½ As.

An imaginary tour round India, with visits to Nepal and Cashmere, describing the principal cities and other objects of interest. With 97 woodcuts illustrative of the Himalayas, Calcutta, Benares, Agra, Delhi, Bombay, Madras, &c

THE PRINCIPAL NATIONS OF INDIA. 8vo. 160 pp. 4 As. Post-free, 5 As.

An account of 42 Nations and Tribes of India, with specimens of some of their languages, and 55 Illustrations.

THE NATIVE STATES OF INDIA AND THEIR PRINCES; WITH NOTICES OF SOME IMPORTANT ZEMINDARIS. 4to. 100 pp. 5 As. Post-free, 6 As.

157 States are described, and 32 portraits are given. The little book will help to enable Indians to understand the vast extent of their country, and what is being one for its improvement.

KASI, OR BENARES, The Holy City of the Hindus. Imperial 8vo. 44 pp. 3 As. Post-free, 4 As.

An account of the city; its Sanskrit schools, ghats, temples, and pilgrimages; with 23 illustrations.

BURMA AND THE BURMESE. 4to. 54 pp. 2½ As. Post-free, 3 As.

A description of the manners and customs of the Burmese; an account of their government, religion, and history, with illustrative woodcuts, and portraits of King Theebaw and his Queen.

LANKA AND ITS PEOPLE; or, A DESCRIPTION OF CEYLON. 4to. 72 pp. 3 As. Post-free, 3½ As.

The account of Lanka given in the Ramayana is first mentioned. Its history, and present condition are then described, with numerous illustrative woodcuts.

PICTORIAL TOUR ROUND ENGLAND, SCOTLAND AND IRELAND. Imperial 8vo. 114 pp. 6 As. Post-free, 7½ As.

Description of the chief places of interest; Public Schools and Universities; Coal Mines and Manufactures; the British Government; Home Life; England an example and warning to India. With 104 woodcuts, and coloured engraving of the Queen-Empress.

PICTURES OF CHINA AND ITS PEOPLE. 4to. 56 pp. 2½ As. Post-free, 3 As.

Extent, History, Manners and Customs of the People; Schools, Examinations; Industries; Travelling Language and Literature; Government; Religions; India and China compared; with 64 Illustrations.

JAPAN: THE LAND OF THE RISING SUN. 4to. 68 pp. 2½ As. Post-free, 3 As.

With 49 illustrations. An interesting description of this beautiful country, and an account of the remarkable changes which have taken place in it.

PICTORIAL TOUR ROUND BIBLE LANDS, Imperial 8vo. 100 pp. 6 As. Post-free, 7½ As.

The principal countries mentioned in the Bible and in ancient history are described; as, Palestine, Syria, Babylon, Asia Minor, Greece and Italy; with 104 illustrations.

ARABIA, AND ITS PROPHET. 4to. 64 pp. 2½ As. Post-free, 3 As.

An account of the Arabs; with descriptions of Jeddah, Mecca, Medina; the History of Muhammad and the early Caliphs; the Koran, Muslim Doctrines, Sects, Prayers, Pilgrimage, &c. with numerous illustrations.

PICTURES OF RUSSIA AND ITS PEOPLES. Imperial 8vo. 83 pp. 5 As. Post-free, 6 As.

A description both of European and Asiatic Russia, including an account of the different races by which they are peopled, their manners and customs, the Government, &c.; with 39 illustrations and maps.

PICTURES OF WOMEN IN MANY LANDS. Imperial 8vo. 112 pp. 6 As. Post-free, 7½ As.

Descriptions of women, beginning with the most degraded nations of the world, and gradually ascending to the most enlightened; with suggestions, from the review, for Indian women, 172 illustrations.

Biographies.

STATESMEN OF RECENT TIMES. 8vo. 192 pp. 8 As. Post-free, 9½ As.

Accounts are given of the leading Statesmen in the great countries of the world; as Gladstone, Salisbury, Bismarck and others. Special notice is taken of those interested in India. In all 182 are mentioned, with 122 portraits.

THE GOVERNORS-GENERAL OF INDIA, First Series. By Henry Morris, M. C. S. (Retired) 8vo. 144 pp. 4 As. Post-free, 5 As.

Contains sketches of the lives of Warren Hastings, Lord Cornwallis, Sir John Shore, Marquis Wellesley, the Earl of Minto, and the Marquis of Hastings, with portraits. Interesting personal details are given, such as are not usually found in histories.

ANGLO-INDIAN WORTHIES: By Henry Morris, Madras C. S. (Retired.) 8vo. 160 pp. 4 As. Full cloth, gilt title, 10 As.

Lives of Sir Thomas Munro, Sir John Malcolm, Lord Metcalfe, Mountstuart Elphinstone, James Thomason, Sir Henry Lawrence, Sir James Outram, Sir Donald Macleod, and Sir Bartle Frere, with portraits.

EMINENT FRIENDS OF MAN; or, LIVES OF DISTINGUISHED PHILANTHROPISTS. 8vo. 158 pp. 4 As. Post-free, 5 As. Full cloth, gilt title, 10 As.

Sketches of Howard, Oberlin, Granville Sharp, Clarkson, Wilberforce, Buxton, Pounds, Davies of Devauden, George Moore, Montefiore, Livesey, the Earl of Shaftesbury, and others; with remarks on what might be done in India.

SOME NOTED INDIANS OF MODERN TIMES. 8vo. 164 pp. 4 As. Post-free, 5 As.

Sketches of Indian Religious and Social Reformers, Philanthropists, Scholars, Statesmen, Judges, Journalists, and others, with several portraits.

MARTIN LUTHER, THE GREAT EUROPEAN REFORMER. 8vo. 109 pp. 2½ As. Post-free, 3 As.

The state of religion in Europe in the time of Luther is described; a full account is given of his undaunted efforts to bring about a reformation; the greater need of a similar change in India is shown, and Luther is held up as an example. 15 Illustrations.

BABA PADMANJI. An Autobiography. 8vo. 108 pp. 2½ As. Post-free, 3 As.

An interesting account by himself of this popular Marathi author, describing his conversion from Hinduism to Christianity.

PICTURE STORIES OF NOBLE WOMEN. 4to. 50 pp. 2½ As. Post-free, 3 As.

Account of Cornelia, Agrippina, Padmani of Chittore, Lady Jane Grey, Ahaliya Bai, Mrs. Fry, Princess Alice, Miss Carpenter, Maharani Surnomayi, Pandita Ramabai, Miss Nightingale, and Lady Dufferin.

THE QUEEN-EMPRESS OF INDIA AND HER FAMILY. 43 pp. 3 As. Post-free, 3½ As.

Her early life; marriage; widowhood; children: progress in India during her reign; traits of character and lessons from her life. With 27 illustrations, and a coloured portrait of the Empress.

☞ *See also the Anna Library.*

The Anna Library. 1 Anna, each.

Mostly with Numerous Illustrations.

INDIAN FABLES. 48 pp.
PICTURE FABLES. 48 pp.
CHOICE PICTURES AND STORIES. 48 pp.
PICTURES AND STORIES FOR THE YOUNG. 48 pp.

Saint Augustine, the greatest Early Christian Writer.
William Carey. 48 pp.
Story of Dr. Livingstone. 48 pp.
Story of Dr. Duff, by A. L. O. E. 56 pp.
Thomas Arnold, the Model English Teacher. 48 pp.
General Garfield. 48 pp.
Neesima: the True Patriot of Japan. 48 pp.
Palissy the Potter. 48 pp.
India in Vedic Times. 48 pp.
Picture Stories of the Ancient Greeks. 48 pp.
Pictures and Stories of the Old Romans. 48 pp.
Picture Stories from English History. 48 pp.
Pictures and Stories of Wild Beasts. 48 pp.
Pictures and Stories of Birds. 48 pp.
Snakes, Crocodiles, and other Reptiles. 48 pp.
Fishes and Whales. 48 pp.
Curious Little People; a Description of Insects. 48 pp.
The Wonderful House I Live in. 48 pp.
A description of the human body.
Astronomy and Astrology. 48 pp.
Burning Mountains, Earthquakes, and other Wonders. 48 pp.
The Ayah and Lady. By Mrs. Sherwood. 64 pp.
Proverbs from East and West. 48 pp.
Buddha and his Religion. 60 pp.
Idols of the Earth: Ancient and Modern. 48 pp.
History of the True Incarnation. 52 pp.
Short Papers for Seekers after Truth. 12mo. 112 pp.
A Guide to Religious Inquirers.
Short Papers for Young Men. 12mo. 104 pp.
A Sequel to the foregoing. Hints on General Conduct, the Choice of a Profession, and Success in Life.

Publications for Students.

Select Convocation Addresses, delivered to Graduates of the Madras University. 8vo. 231 pp. Stiff covers, 8 As.; Half-bound in cloth 12 As. Full bound in cloth, with gilt title, 1 Rupee, Post-free.

The volume contains 15 addresses, commencing in 1859, and including several of the most recent. Some of the most distinguished men in South India during the last 30 years took part in the Series. Many very useful hints to young men entering upon the battle of life in any part of India will be found in the collection.

The Indian Student's Manual. 12mo. 352 pp. 8 As. Post-free, 9 As.

Hints on Studies, Examinations, Moral Conduct, Religious Duties and Success in Life.

S. P. C. K. PRESS, VEPERY, MADRAS—1895.